MY CANCER JOURNEY OF RESILIENCE & SELF-LOVE

Loving Me

FREDDIE HARRIS

Loving Me

Copyright @ 2025 Freddie Harris
ISBN: 979-8-9919922-9-9
All rights reserved.

Author owns complete rights to this book and may be contacted in regards to distribution. Printed in the United States of America.

Library of Congress Cataloging-in-Publication Data

The copyright laws of the United States of America protect this book. No part of this publication may be reproduced or stored in a retrieval system for commercial gain or profit.

No part of this publication may be stored electronically or otherwise transmitted in any form or by any means (electronic, photocopy, recording) without written permission of the author except as provided by USA copyright law. For permissions, contact:

shero. Publishing
SHEROPUBLISHING.COM

Publishing/Editing: SHERO Publishing
Graphics & Cover Design: Greenlight Creations Graphics Designs
glightcreations.com/ glightcreations@gmail.com

Loving Me

Table of Contents

Dedication		4
Preface		6
Acknowledgments		7
Introduction		8

The Journey

Chapter 1	Facing The Diagnosis	12
Chapter 2	Breast or No Breast	20
Chapter 3	Finding Strength, Support & Beauty...	30
Chapter 4	Whispered Battles: Work and Family	38
Chapter 5	Ringing the Bell	42
Chapter 6	The House That Faith Built	46
Chapter 7	The Reoccurrence	52
Chapter 8	Divine Intervention	60
Chapter 9	Juicing Through Adversity...	70
Chapter 10	A Mother's Sacrifice	78
Chapter 11	No Pockets- Identifying a Patient Need	86
Chapter 12	Naked: Finding Purpose in the Pain	92
Chapter 13	Parallel Paths: Stories of Strength	98
Chapter 14	The Blessings Through the Storm	106
AuthorBio	Author Freddie Harris	124

Dedication

This book is lovingly dedicated to the memory of Octavia E. Howard, the woman who inspired and supported me every step of the way.

It serves as a heartfelt tribute to my dear mother, whose enduring inspiration and unwavering support echo through the spirit of *Loving Me* and *Sisters Speak Life*. Though she is no longer physically with us, her legacy of resilience, strength, love, and appreciation for others continues to guide this empowering journey. Through the cherished memories of her presence, we find strength, compassion, and purpose.

This dedication also extends to my brothers, Robert and James, who, like me, were deeply shaped and supported by our beloved mother. May this book stand as a testament to the love, wisdom, and joy she so freely gave, ensuring her spirit remains an eternal source of inspiration for women and individuals walking their unique paths of empowerment.

May the pages of this book not only capture the essence of Octavia E. Howard's love and wisdom but also remind us that her influence lives on in each of us. Her spirit continues to guide and inspire, creating a powerful and uplifting story for everyone who joins this journey through these words.

With deep gratitude for the enduring legacy, she bestowed upon us, we, her children, embrace the path ahead, carrying her light in our hearts.

With love and reverence,
Freddie Ann Harris

Preface

As a child, I was so scared of caterpillars. I thought they were the ugliest, most alarming creatures ever, and I would jump and dodge to avoid them. But during my tough battle with breast cancer, I found comfort and inspiration in the most unexpected place.

It's strange to think that the very creature that once made me scramble in fear—the caterpillar—has now become a symbol of strength and beauty for me. Watching it transform into a butterfly showed me how much resilience I had. Oh, what beauty there is in the butterfly, with its wings showing off transformation and grace.

Like the caterpillar, I went through my own big transformation during this journey. I came out of the darkness of diagnosis and treatment with new courage and self-love.

This shared journey of transformation inspired the name *Loving Me,* capturing the essence of my journey towards self-love and acceptance.

Acknowledgements

As I close this chapter of my journey, I am overwhelmed with gratitude for the many hearts and hands that helped bring *Loving Me* to life. This book is more than words on a page—it is a testament to love, resilience, and the power of faith.

In loving memory of my father, Robert Howard Sr., who, though gone too soon, left me with the gift of unconditional love that continues to live within me. And to my uncle JD, whose strength and support were a source of comfort and guidance.

To my family—thank you for being my foundation, my strength, and my greatest blessing.

To my church family—thank you for your prayers, encouragement, and unwavering faith in God's power to heal and restore.

To my friends and community—thank you for your encouragement and belief in me, even when the road was difficult.

To my medical team—thank you for your care, compassion, and dedication to my healing. You were the hands and hearts behind each step of my recovery.

To the survivors, caregivers, and warriors—your resilience is the heartbeat of this story. May this book serve as a testament to your strength and a beacon of encouragement.

May we continue to stand together, with courage in our hearts and hope in our souls, knowing that true healing begins with loving ourselves.

Introduction

Once again, I found myself in a cold, sterile waiting room. For years, I had sat in rooms like this, first at Maria Parham Medical Center and later at Duke Cancer Center. The rhythm of mammograms and screenings had become a routine part of my life since my first breast cancer diagnosis in 2001, when I heard the words "You have breast cancer. I still remember the fear that consumed me and the long road of treatment that followed. Then came 2008, when I was blindsided by a second diagnosis—one that tested every ounce of my faith and resilience. Each time, I faced a battle I never wanted, but I emerged stronger, carried by faith, family, and the quiet assurance of the Holy Spirit, my sweet constant companion.

But today, something felt different. It was November 2020, and as I sat in the waiting room at Duke Medical Center for my yearly mammogram, the air seemed thicker, almost suffocating. The familiar sounds—the hum of fluorescent lights, the shuffle of footsteps in the hallway—felt magnified, echoing in the stillness of the room.

The space itself was designed to be calming, with pale walls, pastel-colored artwork, and rows of identical chairs. Yet, nothing could ease the tension that hung in the air. Earlier, the nurse had guided me through the familiar steps: handing me a gown, directing me to change, and walking me through the mammogram. Now, I was back in the waiting room, clutching the thin fabric of my gown like a shield, anxiously awaiting the results.

There were two doors in this waiting room.
One to the right and one to the left.

The door to the right brought good news: a nurse would step out with a paper in hand, signaling that everything was clear, and I could go home with the promise of returning in a year. But the door to the left meant they had identified an area of concern, and further testing was needed. It meant more waiting and the kind of uncertainty that had defined too many moments of my life.

Around me, other women sat quietly, each one lost in her own thoughts. Some tapped their fingers nervously against the armrests, while others whispered prayers into cupped hands. One by one, they were called through one of the two doors ahead.

I watched as the room emptied, leaving me alone. I stared at the left door, willing it to stay closed. My heart pounded in my chest as the minutes stretched into what felt like hours.

And then, it opened.

The door to the left.

The nurse called my name, and my heart sank. The wallpaper blurred around me as my chest tightened, and the familiar lump in my throat grew heavier.

Before I share what happened next, let me take you back to where it all began in 2001. My journey is not just about the challenges I faced but also about the incredible blessings I discovered along the way. Through journaling, I found healing, strength, and a deeper connection with God.

As you read my story, I invite you to reflect on your own journey. How has God shown up for you in your moments of uncertainty? I hope that by sharing my experiences, you find renewed strength, hope, and the realization that even in the midst of life's storms, blessings are all around us—if we take the time to see them.

MY CANCER JOURNEY OF RESILIENCE & SELF-LOVE

Loving Me

FREDDIE HARRIS

Chapter 1

Chapter 1:
Facing the Diagnosis

The Discovery

As I lay in bed one restless night, tossing and turning in my attempt to quit smoking, a sudden unrest gripped me. The weight of a pack-a-day habit bore down on me heavily. In a moment of absentminded self-reflection, my fingers grazed something unfamiliar—a cluster of fine bumps on my left breast. Startled, I froze. I hadn't noticed them before.

A mix of fear and anxiety settled over me like a heavy fog. I clung to the hope that it was nothing, but the worry refused to let me rest. My annual OB/GYN appointment was just two days away, and those bumps lingered in my thoughts, casting shadows over my sleepless nights.

When the day of my appointment arrived, I wasted no time in confiding in Estena, my Nurse Practitioner. Her response was swift and decisive, a testament to her dedication and expertise. With calm urgency, she examined me and sprang into action without hesitation. Before I knew it, she had scheduled a mammogram and arranged a consultation with Dr. Joe, a highly respected breast surgeon renowned for his expertise.

The sense of urgency only grew stronger as the day of my appointment approached, each passing moment fueling a mix of apprehension and determination. Although I trusted and believed I was in capable hands, the unknown weighed heavily on me.

When I met with Dr. Joe, a series of tests were initiated: diagnostic mammograms, breast ultrasounds and needle biopsies. Each step brought me closer to an answer I wasn't ready to hear. Each visit intensified the reality of the situation. After the initial tests, Dr. Joe made a simple yet heavy request: *"Bring someone with you to discuss the results."*

At first, I brushed it off. *"I've got this,"* I told myself. But deep down, I knew better. It took the gentle nudging of my best friend, Mary Frances, and the unwavering support of my mother to convince me otherwise. Together, they accompanied me to the appointment.

Dr. Joe called us into his office. With my mother and Mary Frances sitting beside me, he delivered the words I had been dreading: *"The biopsy came back cancerous."*

Time seemed to stop. I heard him talking, but I couldn't process the details. The room felt small, the air thick. My thoughts froze, my breath shallow.

The car ride home was silent, the weight of the diagnosis sitting with us like an uninvited guest. The hum of the engine filled the space where words should have been. My mind raced, trying to make sense of it all.

It was during that quiet drive that the reason Dr. Joe insisted I bring someone with me became painfully clear. He knew the weight of those words would be too much to carry alone.

Almost in unison, my mother and I turned to Mary Frances and asked, *"What did he say?"* With calm strength, Mary Frances repeated what neither of us could fully accept: *"The biopsy showed cancer."* Her words lingered in the air, settling into a truth we were just beginning to process.

The Next Phase

After hearing the biopsy results, I was faced with a critical decision: a lumpectomy to remove the cancerous tissue or a mastectomy to remove the entire breast. Dr. Joe walked me through the options, explaining the procedures and their implications. Ultimately, I chose to have a lumpectomy, determined to fight this cancer one step at a time.

When I first received my diagnosis, it felt as if my whole world had collapsed. I tried to stay strong for my family, especially my mother, but inside, *the tempest was raging.* I was consumed by anger and confusion. I had just gone through a tough divorce after 17 years of marriage, and now this—breast cancer.

For days, I cried silently, unable to comprehend how I would navigate this storm. I was angry at everything—at myself, at the world. *Why me?* I asked repeatedly, but no answer ever came.

Nights were the hardest. I'd lie awake, tears streaming down my face, feeling as if I were drowning in fear and uncertainty.

It was during one of my counseling sessions with Pastor Joann that I began to unravel these emotions. She listened patiently as I shared the anger, I felt from both the diagnosis and the failed marriage. Her words were a balm to my wounded soul. She advised me to refocus on the battle ahead, to forgive my ex-husband and, more importantly, to forgive myself. She reminded me of the importance of surrounding myself with positive, supportive people.

At first, I struggled to process her advice, but I realized that holding onto anger was only making me weaker in the fight against cancer. Letting go of resentment and pain became necessary. When people asked what had happened in my marriage, my response became simple and honest: *We failed to work out our differences.* This statement reflected a place of acceptance and understanding, free from blame and bitterness.

Slowly, I began to see that my journey wasn't just about surviving; it was about finding purpose in the midst of chaos.

As I continued to pray and call out to God, something within me began to shift. I can't fully explain it, but it felt as if a light broke through the darkness—a glimmer of hope appeared amidst the despair. Peace washed over me—a peace I couldn't fully understand but deeply felt. With trembling hands and a shaky voice, I asked God, *"What do you want me to do with this?"*

In the quiet of my heart, I felt an answer—not in words, but in a profound sense of comfort and reassurance. I wasn't alone. I clung to a verse that became my anchor:

"For I know the plans I have for you," declares the Lord, *"plans to prosper you and not to harm you, plans to give you hope and a future."* (Jeremiah 29:11)

Despite the uncertainty, despite the fear, I chose to keep moving forward. And with every step, I embraced the journey, knowing that my story could be a beacon of hope for others. My pain became my purpose. My struggle became a testament to resilience.

Even in our darkest moments, there is always a glimmer of light, a reason to keep fighting, and a story worth sharing.

The New Adversary: As if Divorce Wasn't Hard Enough!

Never would I have imagined encountering breast cancer after surviving a divorce—a chapter of my life filled with its own trials and heartbreaks.

Fresh out of college with a degree in Radio-TV and Film Communications, I embarked on an exciting career. My first job was a dream come true—working as a weather radio announcer at the National Weather Service in Raleigh, NC, thanks to a partnership between my alma mater, Shaw University, and the National Weather Service. I still remember the excitement of my first broadcast, my heart racing as my voice reached thousands of listeners, delivering vital weather updates.

In the midst of my growing career, love found its way into my life. I said, "I do," and with that, a new adventure began. Marriage led me back to my hometown of Henderson, NC. After completing additional courses, I transitioned into social work in Child Welfare services. This shift ignited my passion for making a difference in the lives of children and families.
But life had other plans.

After 17 years of marriage, my relationship—once filled with hope and happiness—came to a heartbreaking end. The nights were long and filled with tears, but I was determined to rebuild my life. I yearned for stability, believing the worst was behind me, and looked forward to embracing my newfound independence.

I refused to let the pain define me. I leaned into new opportunities, balancing my work in Child Welfare services while earning my real estate license. The fast-paced industry provided a welcome distraction, a fresh start, and a financial lifeline as I adjusted to life on a single income. Just as I was beginning to regain my footing, fate had another test in store—breast cancer.

Cancer was an uninvited adversary that shook me to my core. Divorce had tested my resilience, but this was a battle unlike any other. The illusion of stability I had fought so hard to reclaim was suddenly shattered. Yet through the fear and uncertainty, my faith became my anchor, teaching me the true meaning of courage and self-love.

Despite never discussing cancer openly, its presence loomed largely in my family's medical history—a silent legacy that would soon shape my own journey in ways I never anticipated. Little did I know, this encounter with death would become a recurring theme in my life's narrative.

But even the most painful endings can lead to new beginnings, and even the darkest nights can reveal a guiding light.

Chapter 2

Chapter 2:
Breast or No Breast:

Breast or No Breast

Although I found myself at a crossroads, the decision had already been made—I would have the lumpectomy. Thinking back, how do you make a decision when every option feels like a loss?

For me, the answer came through faith, trust, and the support of those around me. It wasn't a single moment of clarity but a process—one where I leaned on my loved ones, my faith, and prayer. I had to remind myself that making the "right" decision didn't mean eliminating all uncertainty but choosing the best path forward with the information and strength I had at the time. With each step, I found the courage to move forward, even when the way wasn't clear.

The Weight of the Decision

The word cancer had shattered my world, forcing me into a decision I never imagined I'd have to make: lumpectomy or mastectomy. The very thought of removing my entire breast sent shivers down my spine. It felt like more than just a medical decision—it was a question of survival and how I would see myself moving forward.

During my silent struggle, I came to acknowledge the truth—strength is not found in hiding but in the willingness to share the load with others. For days, I wept in silence, convinced that vulnerability was a frailty best concealed. Fear whispered that I should handle this alone, and shame crept in, making me wonder if I was weak for breaking down. Yet, in the depths of despair, I realized that true fortitude lies not in the absence of tears, but in the bravery to shed them in the company of others.

As a newly divorced woman, the fear wasn't just about my health—it was about my future. Would I ever feel whole again? Would anyone love me, scars and all? Cancer wasn't just attacking my body; it was attacking my sense of femininity and identity. Beyond my personal fears, I worried about my mother and family. I couldn't bear to see them in pain, so I did what I had always done—I masked my own. I smiled through the uncertainty, determined to be strong even as doubt consumed me.

Making the Choice

Even though Dr. Joe explained my options, I was still lost. I replayed the possibilities in my mind, searching for certainty where none existed. What if I made the wrong choice? What if my decision didn't give me the best chance at survival?

I was afraid—not just of cancer, but of what it would take away from me. I was already rebuilding my life after divorce, and now this. Would I ever recognize the woman in the mirror again?

A Defining Encounter with God

In my lowest moments, I turned to my faith, remembering that quiet encounter with God. In the stillness of that night, something shifted. A deep sense of peace settled over me—not the absence of fear, but the reassurance that I wasn't alone.

With that peace, I was able to make the decision. I would choose the lumpectomy. I wanted to preserve as much of my body as possible, hoping that a lumpectomy would allow me to hold on to a part of myself. The idea of removing my entire breast felt like too much, too final. My doctors assured me that with chemotherapy and radiation, a lumpectomy was a viable option. I held on to that reassurance, believing that this path would not only give me a chance at survival but also help me maintain a sense of normalcy in a life that felt anything but normal.

Moving Forward with Purpose

With faith and the support of my mother and family, I underwent five rounds of chemotherapy every 21 days, followed by six weeks of radiation, five days a week. Each treatment tested me, but I kept going.

This experience marked the beginning of a journey that tested me in ways I could never have imagined but also revealed strengths and blessings I hadn't yet discovered. Perhaps the weight of the situation made it difficult to ask the right questions, or maybe we were simply too afraid to think beyond the immediate plan. Either way, we moved forward with what felt like the best course of action at the time.

The Cannonball Moment

I recall my first chemotherapy treatment, sitting in the recliner as the nurse prepped my IV. My heart pounded, my body tense. I didn't know what to expect, only that everything about this felt unnatural—this wasn't supposed to be my life.

Then, the nurse looked at me and said, "You look like you've been shot out of a cannon."

And that's exactly what I felt like.

A cannonball flying through the air at 1,000 miles per hour, weightless yet crushingly heavy at the same time. I was hurtling forward, bracing for an impact I couldn't see, gripping onto faith because it was the only thing I had left.

As the IV dripped the first dose of chemo into my veins, a cool sensation spread through my arm. A slight metallic taste settled on my tongue—something I had heard about but didn't expect to notice so quickly. (Later, Mary Francis gave me lemon drop candy that helped to mask the taste) My stomach tensed slightly, a mix of nerves and the unfamiliar effects of the medication. I could feel the medicine working its way through my body, a quiet but firm reminder that this was the beginning of a fight I had no choice but to face.

Alongside the physical effects came a new wave of emotions. Shame, uncertainty, and fear tangled together, weighing me down. I had always been the strong one, the one who held things together. But here I was, weak, vulnerable, and exposed in a way I never imagined. I wanted to hide, to retreat into myself, but there was no escape. I had to face this, even if I didn't feel ready.

Again, I had to draw my strength from that night when Jeremiah 29:11 was dropped into my spirit—

"For I know the plans I have for you," declares the Lord, "plans to prosper you and not to harm you, plans to give you hope and a future."

I clung to that promise, whispering it in my heart as the IV dripped chemo into my veins. This journey wasn't just about surviving; it was about trusting that even in my fear, even in my uncertainty, God had already planned my future.

A New Understanding of Strength

In embracing my struggle with compassion and kindness toward myself, I found resilience. In confronting my pain with self-acceptance, I discovered purpose. Learning to be vulnerable allowed me to connect more deeply with myself and others. It was in those moments of honesty—when I acknowledged both my fear and my faith—that I found the strength to keep going.

My story was no longer just about enduring breast cancer. It became a testament to faith, self-love, and the unbreakable strength of the human spirit.

But while I had come to terms with this battle, I didn't yet realize that cancer wasn't finished with me. There were still lessons to learn, scars to embrace, and an even deeper strength waiting to be uncovered.

The Day I Lost My Hair: A Moment of Empowerment

Losing my hair was an expected side effect of chemotherapy—something I knew would happen, yet I dreaded all the same. About a month after my first session, the signs began to show. My dear friends Liz, Linnoya, and Bridgette and I had already devised a plan for this moment. We figured that if I cut my hair before it fell out completely, it would give me a sense of control over something that felt so wildly out of my hands.

One morning, as I rubbed my head, I noticed loose strands collecting in my fingers. A knot tightened in my chest as I realized what this meant. I took a deep breath and picked up the phone, calling each of my friends and simply saying, *"It's time."* Those two words carried so much weight, and on the other end of the line, I could hear the quiet understanding in their voices. This was a moment we'd prepared for, but now it was real.

The ride to Simply Bridgette's Salon was quiet, heavy with unspoken emotions. My friends were with me, their presence steadying me as I tried to brace myself. I looked out the window, watching the world carry on as if everything was normal. But for me, this wasn't just a car ride—it felt like a journey into a new chapter of my life. A chapter where I'd confront the mirror and see a version of myself, I wasn't sure I was ready to meet.

When we arrived, the gravity of the moment truly hit me. My heart felt heavy with fear, sadness, and a profound sense of loss. I had always taken pride in my hair—the regular hairdos, the way I kept it styled just right. Now, all of that was about to change. I thought I was prepared, but sitting in the salon chair, I realized nothing could fully prepare me for this.

Bridgette, in her calm and caring way, led me to a private room, making the moment feel intimate and sacred. She began by sectioning my hair with gentle hands, pulling each piece aside with a respect that felt almost ceremonial.

The room grew still, almost reverent, as if we both understood the weight of every snip that was about to happen.

I watched the first pieces of hair fall onto the cape, drifting to the floor. Each strand felt like more than just hair—it was a piece of me, a part of my identity, that I was letting go. Tears rolled down my cheeks, a quiet way of saying goodbye to what was being left behind.

Finally, the last strands were shaved away, and I lifted my eyes to the mirror. Staring back at me was a smooth, bare scalp—a look I had never imagined for myself. My skin was pale and tender, almost vulnerable, like a blank canvas where my hair once was. And yet, as I took in this new reflection, something surprising began to stir within me—a quiet strength.

In that moment, I realized this was more than just a haircut. It was an act of courage. It was a choice—a way of reclaiming some control in a process that often left me feeling powerless. I wasn't just losing my hair; I was choosing to let it go on my own terms.

When I looked in the mirror again, I felt an unexpected sense of relief. My head felt lighter, both physically and emotionally. I had taken charge of something that had seemed uncontrollable, and in doing so, I reclaimed a part of myself. This wasn't just a haircut; it was a moment of empowerment. I was letting go of my need to cling to every piece of who I was before. I was ready to face whatever came next.

As we prepared to leave, Linnoya handed me a straw hat she had brought for me, and I smiled at her thoughtfulness. On the ride home, the conversation turned lighthearted. We laughed and talked about bold lipstick shades, oversized earrings, and all the ways I could embrace my new look. This wasn't just about loss anymore— it was about discovery. In that moment, surrounded by love and laughter, I realized that even in the hardest seasons, there's always room for small joys and moments of beauty.

Sunday Morning: Losing My Hair

They say something always happens on a Sunday morning when you're getting ready for church—you can't find your shoes, the car keys disappear, or your stockings suddenly have a run. Sunday mornings have their own kind of chaos, but this Sunday was different.

While I had expected to lose my hair, I hadn't given any thought to losing my eyelashes and eyebrows. That morning, as I prepared for church, I stood in front of the mirror trying to wrap one of the scarves that Pastor Joann had lovingly gifted me. Just the day before, I had been at a small shop where a kind woman patiently taught me how to tie them. She encouraged me, reassured me, and sent me on my way feeling prepared.

But now, as I tried to recreate those wraps, nothing felt right. My hands fumbled, and the scarf refused to cooperate. I was growing anxious and sweating as the clock ticked closer to church time. I paused to look at myself in the mirror, trying to calm down—and that's when I noticed it. My eyelashes and eyebrows were gone.

It felt like a gut punch. I hadn't realized this would happen, and the sight of my face without those defining features brought me to tears. I cried—not just because I wanted hair, eyebrows and eyelashes, but for all the little pieces of myself that felt like they were slipping away. I cried for the woman in the mirror who didn't look like me.

But even in those tears, something shifted. I wasn't going to let this moment defeat me. I wiped my face, drew on my eyebrows, lined my eyes the best I could, and pressed forward. The scarf was abandoned, and I walked out of the house bare headed. It wasn't easy, but it was necessary. I couldn't let this moment define me.

When I arrived at church, I was late. Instead of slipping quietly through the side door into the choir loft, I walked boldly through the front. Pastor Joann's voice rang out as she led the choir in, "Lord, Do It." As she reached the line, "*Do it for me, Lord,*" the words filled the sanctuary, wrapping around me. It felt like a direct plea from my heart to God. Every word felt like a lifeline.

I could have collapsed at the altar right then and there, overcome by the weight of the moment. But I kept walking, my head held high, my faith carrying me forward.

By the time I joined the choir stand, something had changed in me. Singing alongside my choir family, I felt lighter, stronger. The scripture Philippians 4:13 echoed in my spirit:

"I can do all things through Christ who strengthens me."

That day, I realized something powerful: my strength wasn't in my hair, my lashes, or my brows. My strength was in my faith, my resilience, and the God who had been walking with me every step of the way. I was still me—*still Freddie*—still whole. And no matter how many pieces I might lose along this journey, nothing could take away the strength God had placed within me.

Chapter 3

Chapter 3:
Finding Strength, Support & Beauty in Unexpected Places

My passage through breast cancer was an emotional roller-coaster, marked by peaks of hope and valleys of fear. Yet, amidst the uncertainty, I discovered reservoirs of strength and resilience within myself that I never knew existed. The timeless wisdom of scripture became my steadfast companion during this tumultuous time. Sheets of scripture, provided by Pastor Joann, adorned the mirrors of my home, serving as constant reminders of God's presence and promise.

In moments of doubt and despair, Psalm 23 became my refuge—a comforting assurance that, even in the darkest valleys, I was not alone. The imagery of the Lord as my shepherd, guiding me with His rod and staff, provided solace and renewed strength to face each day.

Reflecting on my journey, I'm overwhelmed with gratitude for the unwavering support that buoyed me through the darkest of days. Within the embrace of my mother, family, friends, and community, I found solace, and through the kindness of strangers, I discovered hope. Despite the uncertainty of the road ahead, I walked with my head held high, fortified by the knowledge that I am never alone.

Isaiah 41:10 became my mantra—a reminder that, even in moments of weakness and fear, God was my source of strength, upholding me with His righteous hand. His words served as my anchor, grounding me in the assurance that I could face whatever lay ahead with courage and resilience.

When the doctor delivered the diagnosis, it felt as if the ground had shifted beneath my feet. Fear and doubt threatened to overwhelm me, but the unwavering support of my loved ones became my anchor. Their presence served as a beacon of hope in my darkest moments, reminding me that I was not alone in this fight.

One particular moment stands out—a moment of divine intervention that left me awestruck. In the depths of despair, I stumbled upon Jeremiah 29:11, where God promises plans to prosper and offer hope for the future. In that moment, I felt a sense of peace wash over me, knowing that God's plans for me transcended my own and that He was working all things together for my good.

Reflecting on my journey, I'm reminded of the words of Romans 8:28, where we're assured that God works for the good of those who love Him. In the tapestry of my breast cancer journey, I see the hand of God weaving a story of redemption and grace—a testament to His enduring presence and unwavering love amidst the ashes of despair.

Prayers of Comfort & Protection:

Psalm 23 (NIV): *The LORD is my shepherd, I lack nothing. He makes me lie down in green pastures, he leads me beside quiet waters, he refreshes my soul. He guides me along the right paths for his name's sake. Even though I walk through the darkest valley, I will fear no evil, for you are with me; your rod and your staff, they comfort me.*

You prepare a table before me in the presence of my enemies. You anoint my head with oil; my cup overflows. Surely your goodness and love will follow me all the days of my life, and I will dwell in the house of the LORD forever.

Isaiah 41:10 (NIV): *So, do not fear, for I am with you; do not be dismayed, for I am your God. I will strengthen you and help you; I will uphold you with my righteous right hand.*

Jeremiah 29:11 (NIV): *For I know the plans I have for you, declares the LORD, plans to prosper you and not to harm you, plans to give you hope and a future.*

Romans 8:28 (NIV): *And we know that in all things God works for the good of those who love him, who have been called according to his purpose.*

Glimmers of Joy

During the challenging time of losing my hair due to chemotherapy, I was feeling particularly tired one day. My mother suggested we take a ride to lift my spirits. We decided to visit my nephew, Corey, and his family. As we entered my nephew's home, the weight of my journey felt heavy on my shoulders.

I had a heartwarming encounter with my 4-year-old great-niece, Jasmine. I am certain her parents had prepared her for my hair loss, telling her that Auntie didn't have hair and not to say anything. Little Jasmine, however, was eagerly awaiting my arrival, practically bouncing with excitement for me to visit her room.

With the innocence and honesty only a child could muster, Jasmine grabbed my hand and led me to her room, her enthusiasm bringing a smile to my face. She eagerly ushered me to her bed, insisting I take a seat beside her. As I settled in, she placed her tiny hand on top of mine, her eyes sparkling with curiosity and kindness.

Then, with a seriousness that belied her age, she looked up at me and uttered those precious words: *"You look pretty."* Tears welled up in my eyes as I thanked her, my heart swelling with gratitude for her pure, unfiltered affection.

I couldn't help but chuckle at her next observation. With a tilt of her head, Jasmine examined my head, squinting slightly as if scrutinizing a puzzle. And then, with the confidence of a seasoned detective, she declared, *"I can see it growing back!"*

In that moment, as I exchanged smiles with this little beacon of light, I was reminded that beauty lies not in the presence or absence of hair, but in the love and laughter shared between us. Jasmine's simple, heartfelt words had the power to uplift my spirit in a way I never expected. This encounter with Jasmine reaffirmed my belief in the wisdom and purity of children, as echoed in the Bible. Their untainted perspectives and boundless love serve as a reminder of the simple yet profound truths in life. Just as Jesus welcomed and blessed the children, we too should cherish and learn from their innocent hearts.

Journey of Strength and Liberation: A Tribute to Bridgette Hawkins

After each round of chemo, my body would be racked with pain for days. The powerful concoction, designed to attack the cancer cells, felt like poison coursing through my veins, leaving me weak and aching. Each treatment was a brutal battle, stripping away my energy and leaving me feeling like a shell of myself. Just as I would begin to feel a glimmer of normalcy, regaining a bit of strength and hope, it would be time for another round, plunging me back into the cycle of pain and exhaustion.

Some days the pain was so excruciating that I believed laying still and not moving was my only option. On those days, Ma would sit beside my bed and spoon-feed me her "Chicken Love Soup." The warmth and love in every spoonful nourished me enough to get up. Often while lying there, my mind would be filled with thoughts of all the things I would do when I got up. I always believed that I would get up because I had to believe it. Driving "Baby Girl" was one of the things I would do.

During one particularly hopeful moment, I devised a plan to embark on a shopping excursion out of state. Convincing my cousin Bridgette to join me, I envisioned a getaway filled with leisurely strolls through malls, delightful dinners, and comfortable accommodations.

When the day came, I gathered every ounce of strength and made my way to "Baby Girl," my trusted vehicle. Neuropathy made each step a challenge, causing me to shuffle my feet, but the mere thought of reaching the truck spurred me forward. With determination, I grasped the steering wheel and pulled myself up into the vehicle, finding solace in the familiar embrace of its interior.

Upon arriving at Bridgette's, I discovered that she had planned to drive and chauffeur me. Bridgette driving never entered my mind as I lay in bed formulating this plan. Eventually, I convinced Bridgette that driving was my best attribute these days. With her kind heart and understanding nature, Bridgette agreed, and we set off on our adventure.

As "Baby Girl" glided down highway 85, I felt the wind rushing through the open windows, casting all my cares aside. The rhythmic hum of the tires against the pavement blended seamlessly with the soulful tunes playing on the radio. I felt renewed, not like a cancer patient, but like a free spirit on an adventure. The open road stretched out before us, a symbol of the endless possibilities that lay ahead. I relished the feeling of independence, knowing that I was doing something on my own, something that made me feel alive and invigorated.

When we arrived in Virginia, we checked into the Hampton Inn and headed straight for the mall. At the mall, I wasn't familiar with the electric carts, but they were a welcome relief. The cart proved to be a blessing, offering respite for my dwindling energy levels. Despite feeling guilty for the challenge, it posed for Bridgette to keep up with me and the electric cart, I reveled in the joy of the moment, grateful for the opportunity to experience life beyond the confines of illness. The simple act of driving and the sense of freedom it brought was a reminder of my strength and resilience- life beyond illness.

Philippians 4:13: *"I can do all things through Christ who strengthens me."*

This section is dedicated to **Bridgette Hawkins, "Simply Bridgette,"** *who is now resting with the Lord. Bridgette was not only my cousin but also a dear friend and a source of unwavering support. She will always be remembered with love and gratitude.*

Chapter 4

Chapter 4:
Whispered Battles: Work

The Storm in the Middle of a Storm

Returning to work while undergoing cancer treatments brought challenges I never anticipated. Chemotherapy and radiation left me physically and emotionally drained, making it difficult to manage a full workload. My doctor provided detailed notes recommending restricted hours and adjustments to my responsibilities, specifically advising against unpredictable duties like being on-call, which disrupted the essential rest I needed to heal.

Despite sharing this documentation with my employer, I later discovered they had contacted my physician directly, inquiring about my ability to fulfill my role. That revelation hit hard. I felt a mix of anger, sadness, and a deep sense of betrayal. Despite my transparency, my health and needs were questioned in a way that felt invasive and dismissive of my reality.

While the situation was eventually resolved with mutual understanding, it was not without emotional strain. However, through this experience, I gained a vital lesson: workplace accommodations are not a courtesy—they are a legal right protected under the Americans with Disabilities Act (ADA). They represent respect, fairness, and the dignity every employee deserves, especially during a health crisis.

To every survivor facing similar challenges: know your rights, advocate for your needs, and don't hesitate to seek support. Familiarize yourself with ADA guidelines, communicate clearly with your HR department, and, if necessary, consult legal professionals. Your health and well-being are non-negotiable, and speaking up is both valid and necessary.

Your journey is valuable, and your needs are legitimate. Don't let fear or uncertainty silence your voice. Stand firm, stay informed, and remember—you are not alone in this fight.

For more information on the **Americans with Disabilities Act (ADA)**: https://www.ada.gov/

Americans With Disabilities Act: Information for People Facing Cancer:
https://www.cancer.org/cancer/financial-insurance-matters/health-insurance-laws/americans-with-disabilities-act.html

Chapter 5

Chapter 5:
Ringing the Bell

Celebrating Life's Milestones

After enduring five rounds of chemotherapy and five weeks of daily radiation, the moment had finally arrived—the end of my cancer treatment. To honor this monumental occasion, my high school best friend and sister-in-spirit, Denita, and I decided to create our own celebration.

Denita drove from Laurel, Maryland, to pick me up, and together, we set out on a Thelma-and-Louise-style road trip to Fort Lauderdale, Coconut Grove, and Key West, Florida. With Denita behind the wheel, I allowed myself to fully relax, letting the open road symbolize my newfound freedom.

Choosing to drive instead of fly or take Amtrak was a conscious decision. Amtrak was too slow, and flying? Well, let's just say I prefer being in control. "When I want to pull over, the pilot can't!" I'd joke, imagining the chaos of trying to get a plane to land mid-flight. So, we took the scenic route, relishing the luxury of pulling over whenever the mood struck, savoring every bit of our adventure.

Denita, being the amazing sister she is, not only drove the entire way but also managed to work remotely during the trip. She juggled conference calls and emails, often pulling over to scenic spots to work with a view. Despite her busy schedule, she never made me feel like an afterthought. I often teased her that no one had a better "office" than the Florida coast.

We indulged ourselves with stays at luxurious five-star hotels in Harbor Beach and Coconut Grove. The trip to Key West, crossing the famous Seven Mile Bridge with the ocean stretching endlessly on either side, felt like a personal victory. Having faced fear head-on, that long stretch of bridge felt less like a challenge and more like a breath of fresh air.

The entire road trip was filled with spontaneous detours and delightful surprises. We explored charming small towns, sampled local cuisine, and treated ourselves to spa days. Each stop along the way was a reminder of life's beauty and joy, and I savored every moment.

At the hotels, we were treated like royalty. The turn-down service with chocolates on the pillow was the perfect touch for our celebratory getaway. When I finally rang the bell to mark the end of my treatment, it felt like the closing of a chapter—one filled with struggle but also resilience and strength.

One afternoon, while relaxing on the beach, a bird spotted my bald head and decided to leave a little "gift." I burst into laughter, wondering if it was a sign of good luck or God's gentle nudge to stay out of the sun. After chemotherapy, avoiding too much sun exposure was essential—my skin was more sensitive, making it prone to burns and irritation. The funny moment added a touch of humor to the day, making it even more memorable.

As our trip came to an end, Denita shared a funny story—my mother had called her and said, "I think it's time for Ann to come home." It felt wonderful to know that no matter how far you travel, someone is waiting to welcome you back.

Returning home, I was met with eager anticipation. Knowing that my loved ones were waiting made the trip even more special.

This road trip wasn't just a celebration of the end of treatment; it was a celebration of life itself—filled with love, laughter, and memories that will last a lifetime. It was the perfect way to close one chapter and step into a new, hopeful beginning.

Chapter 6

Chapter 6:
The House That Faith Built

Nearing my seventh year of cancer survivorship, having completed all treatments and achieved remission, a powerful desire to purchase a home ignited within me. I had my eyes on a particular area of town, but my mother, steadfast in her attachment to our current neighborhood, refused to budge. After much prayer and coming to terms with the reality that Ma would not change her mind, I realized that both of us would worry about the other if we lived apart. So, I decided: I would build my house next door to hers. My ex-husband relinquished his right to the land, I began the loan process, and I chose a builder.

Just as I received loan approval, a distressing discovery shook my world: the cancer had returned, presenting a formidable challenge. The news was like a punch to the gut, leaving me breathless and filled with a flood of emotions—fear, anger, sadness, and uncertainty. I found myself grappling with questions and doubts. How could this be happening again? Was all the previous pain and struggle in vain?

In moments of quiet reflection, as I sat alone with my thoughts, I asked myself, *"Whose report are you going to believe?"* Deep down, I knew that my faith was being tested. The weight of the situation felt almost unbearable, but amidst the turmoil, a quiet resolve began to form. I made a conscious decision to place my trust in God, to lean on my faith even when everything felt like it was crumbling around me. It wasn't easy—there were nights when I would silently cry out to the Lord, seeking strength and understanding.

Through sleepless nights and silent tears, I leaned on God for strength, clinging to His promise that nothing is impossible with Him. Therefore, I decided to move forward. Amid chemotherapy's debilitating effects, the sound of construction became my symphony of hope. The rhythmic pounding of hammers, the whirring of saws, and the occasional shouts of workers were more than just noise; they were a melody of progress and promise. Each sound reminded me that even in the darkest moments, faith can lay the foundation for something greater.

Faith was the foundation that held me up—but practical preparations also played a vital role in helping me move forward. I had been enrolled in an Aflac policy for nearly twenty years. For those unfamiliar, Aflac provides supplemental insurance that helps cover unexpected expenses during major health events. I had a cancer policy, and I didn't realize just how critical that decision would become—*not once, but twice.* I relied on it during my first breast cancer diagnosis in 2001, and again during the second. When my health declined and the bills began to pile up, that policy brought real relief. It allowed me to keep moving forward—even while building my home—in the middle of the storm. Each time I needed support, it was there. In that moment, I fully understood what so many already knew: the Duck works. And for me, it worked exactly when I needed it most.

What a blessing! My nephew Cory became a constant presence during construction, offering support and encouragement when I needed it most. He often walked me over to see the progress firsthand, his steady arm guiding me as I marveled at the transformation. These visits were invaluable, allowing me to see my future home taking shape and even make adjustments to the floor plan. I decided to replace the standard tub with a jacuzzi, envisioning how soothing it would feel after a long day or a round of chemo.

As dawn filters softly through the curtains, a gentle smile crosses your face. You picture the home in detail: a cheerful yellow facade with black shutters, white railings wrapping around the porch, and two black rocking chairs waiting for long, peaceful afternoons. Even before the house was complete, I'd already bought a doormat that read, *"Welcome to the House that Faith Built."* It felt like more than just a decoration—it was a testament to resilience, faith, and the promise of new beginnings.

To purchase my first home past the age of fifty, divorced, and amidst battling cancer seemed an impossible feat. But what an awesome God we serve. His promise in Psalm 37:4 rings true: *"Delight yourself in the Lord, and he will give you the desires of your heart."* Despite what the natural eyes could see, I found solace in knowing that nothing is impossible with God. He not only provided shelter but also renewed my spirit with hope and strength to face each day with courage and faith.

If there were concerns about the timing and whether I should financially go through with a home purchase while facing a cancer diagnosis, not a single doubt was expressed, and I continued forward with excitement. I could feel the support around me. Ma and I lived together during this period. As Pastor Clayton later recounted, Ma shared with him, *"Ann (that's what they call me) is building a house, and we are moving next door."* There was never a doubt in my mind that Ma would be my roommate. It was the best decision I could have made, and I believe it was in accordance with God's word to *" "***Honor your father and mother"***—which is the first commandment with a promise—"so that it may go well with you and that you may enjoy long life on the earth."* (Ephesians 6:2-3).

When the time came to move, it was joyful chaos. Ma's house was next door, and we literally carried our clothes across the walkway. My brother/cousins assisted with moving my bedroom set, and all other furniture was purchased either as a gift from Ma or a gift from me to her. What excitement we felt! Our new home was filled with love and anticipation. We received cards from our village of support—friends, family, and even strangers who heard our story. Prayer warriors would pass our names along to others, and soon, cards of encouragement and prayers flooded our mailbox. Each card was a tangible reminder that we were not alone, that a community stood with us on our journey.

We celebrated with a housewarming party, a joyous occasion filled with laughter, food, and shared dreams. Friends and family came together, bringing gifts and blessings for our new home. The air was filled with love and excitement, and the walls of our home seemed to hum with the collective prayers and well-wishes of those who cared for us.

Within several days of the move, we both ended up in the emergency room. I developed mucositis from chemo. Although I knew I wasn't up to the last treatment, I made the decision to take it as scheduled. In my mind, I believed my mother was sick, and it seemed that everyone's focus was on me; I needed that to change the script. Ma never shared what her emergency room diagnosis was. Often, I wished that I pursued that. I think both of us were so delighted to be released and return to our new home, we didn't give it any more thought.

This journey taught me the true meaning of resilience, faith, and love. Through the trials, I discovered a strength within myself I never knew existed and a deeper connection to my faith that guided me through the darkest of times. I am eternally grateful to my family, friends, and community who supported me, and to God for His unwavering presence and guidance.

In the end, the house next door wasn't just a home. It was a testament to faith, love, and the unyielding human spirit. It was the house that faith built, brick by brick, hope by hope.

Chapter 7

Chapter 7:
The Reoccurrence

A Journey to Survival (2008)

Seven years had passed since my initial breast cancer diagnosis. The new year brimmed with excitement and hope—a fresh chapter marked by healing from divorce and triumphant remission. Determined to embrace life fully, I decided to purchase my first home. Building it right next to my mother's house reflected not only my deep love for family but also a commitment to staying close to the woman who had always been my rock.

But on January 17, 2008, everything changed. While attending a work meeting, I bent forward and felt a sizable knot in my breast. Fear gripped me. Memories of my first diagnosis came flooding back as I urgently called my doctor. By January 21st, I was lying on the table for a needle biopsy with Dr. Bob. What I didn't know at the time was that the mass was so dense it bent the first biopsy needle, forcing him to switch instruments!

On January 24, I received the results—*the cancer had returned*. Silent tears streamed for days as I processed the devastating news. Hearing "breast cancer" for the second time felt like the ground had been pulled out from under me. The battle I thought I had won seemed to start all over again, but this time, the weight was heavier. It was as if a dark shadow had returned, casting doubt and fear over my life once again. The initial shock was paralyzing, a cold numbness spreading through my body. I felt betrayed by my own body, as if it had turned against me despite all the treatments, all the hopes, and all the promises of

a future free from this disease.

The first time, I faced cancer with a warrior's spirit, believing that once I conquered it, the nightmare would be over. But now, the return of cancer felt like an insidious thief, stealing my peace of mind and shattering the fragile sense of security I had slowly rebuilt. The uncertainty was overwhelming, and the fear was profound. Questions raced through my mind: *"How bad is it this time? Will I survive this? Can we remove it? How much more can I endure?"*

The emotional toll was compounded by a sense of isolation. The world around me continued on its usual course, oblivious to the storm raging inside me. I had to summon every ounce of strength to face this new reality, knowing the road ahead would be filled with challenges. Yet, amidst the turmoil, a quiet resolve began to form. I knew I had to fight again—not just for myself, but for those who loved and supported me.

Recognizing the gravity of the situation and the potential severity of my recurrence, Dr. Bob, wanted to ensure we left no stone unturned. He referred me to Duke Medical Center for a comprehensive evaluation, believing that a second opinion and advanced imaging would confirm the full extent of the cancer and provide the best path forward. It was a selfless act, the mark of a great doctor who puts patient care above all else. His decision wasn't about ego; it was about giving me the best chance for survival.

When I connected with Duke and began my journey there, I sent flowers to Dr. Bob, a small token of gratitude for his unselfishness and wisdom. His referral changed the course of my care and reinforced an important truth: the quality of a good doctor isn't just in their skill but in their willingness to seek second opinions when it's in the patient's best interest. Extensive scans at Duke confirmed that the cancer was confined to the left breast. A mastectomy emerged as the solitary option to safeguard my life. This time, survival became a conscious choice. The first time, shock dominated, and I fought with limited awareness of alternatives. The second time, armed with knowledge, I actively embraced life, navigating every step of the fight with determination.

On March 20, 2008, I underwent a mastectomy, sacrificing my left breast as part of the battle against the recurring cancer. Initially, the plan was for my release the next morning, but the medical team insisted that I stay overnight due to the extensive nature of the surgery. However, when my surgical doctor joined his team that morning, I shared my longing to return home to my family—the support system waiting for me. I explained that my 78-year-old mother along with my brother James, and his wife Rosa who had traveled from Massachusetts and were eager to care for me.

As I spoke, I saw the concern and compassion in his eyes. Perhaps it was when he reviewed my medical chart—seeing my minimal use of morphine, my independence in getting to the bathroom, and my overall progress. Perhaps it was his recognition of the critical role emotional support plays in recovery. Or perhaps it's simple—God touched his heart. Whatever the reason, he listened not just to my words but to the emotions behind them—the deep yearning to begin my healing surrounded by those who loved me most.

In that moment, his decision felt like more than just a clinical judgment; it felt like an act of humanity. He understood that healing isn't only about addressing the physical body but also about nurturing the mind and spirit. With insight into the importance of emotional well-being, he granted my release. That morning, his choice became as significant to my healing as the surgery itself.

When I returned home to the love and care of my family, I felt the first glimmer of what true recovery could look like. My family's unwavering support reminded me that recovery is never just about the body—it's also about the heart and soul. With each hug, every whispered prayer, and the simple comfort of being home, I began to understand that healing happens when love and faith meet resilience.

Standing in Front of the Mirror

Weeks later, I faced the inevitable reality of adjusting to life post-mastectomy. I had decided not to pursue reconstructive surgery—a procedure that uses implants or tissue to recreate the shape of the breast. While some may choose this option to restore a sense of normalcy, for me, the decision was about focusing on recovery and moving forward without additional medical interventions. It was a personal choice, but one that came with its own set of challenges and adjustments.

Standing in front of the mirror for the first time after surgery was one of the hardest moments. I avoided it at first, afraid of what I might see. I wasn't ready to confront the physical changes, the scars that told the story of a battle I never wanted to fight. When I finally gathered the courage to look, the reflection staring back at me felt unfamiliar. I saw a side of myself I wasn't sure how to embrace, and for a while, I couldn't even bring myself to touch that side of my chest.

There was an invisible barrier between me and my healing. I feared that touching the scars would make the loss feel more real, that it would remind me of what cancer had taken. But as time passed, I realized that healing wasn't just physical—it was emotional and spiritual, too. Little by little, I let myself explore that side of my chest. It wasn't easy at first, but each time I placed my hand there, I felt stronger. The scars didn't just represent loss—they symbolized survival, resilience, and the choice to keep living.

Finding My Fit

Navigating life after surgery brought practical challenges, especially finding prosthetic and mastectomy bras that felt natural and comfortable. When I opened "The Book," a resource given to me at the hospital, I was overwhelmed by unfamiliar terms like "in-network providers" and "out-of-network providers." The book listed service providers who specialized in fitting prosthetics and mastectomy bras, but the process felt intimidating, as if I were searching for something unattainable.

The first prosthetic I tried left me disheartened. It was firm, rigid, and unnatural in texture—far from matching my skin tone. Instead of blending in, it stood out, a stark reminder of the loss I was trying to adapt to. It felt like a poor attempt to replace what cancer had taken, and instead of helping me heal, it made me feel more disconnected from myself. I remember staring at it, wondering how anyone could think this was an acceptable solution. It didn't feel like me—not in texture, appearance, or comfort.

It was my best friend Rosemary who ultimately guided me to a breakthrough. Rosemary, more like a sister than a friend, had always been a source of strength and wisdom. She recommended a boutique in Danville, Virginia, and her advice changed everything. At the boutique, I found not only a wider range of prosthetics but also bras designed for women who had undergone a mastectomy. While the selection for plus-size women was still limited, it offered a little more variety in colors compared to the previous boutiques I had visited. The prosthetics were softer, more natural in texture, and available in a better range of skin tones, which was a relief after the disheartening experiences I'd had elsewhere.

The staff there didn't just offer products; they offered understanding. They listened to my concerns, treated me with care, and helped me feel seen. For the first time, I felt like I was more than just another survivor—they saw me as a whole person.

The boutique became a sanctuary, a place where I felt supported in my journey to rediscover myself. Though Rosemary has now gone on to be with the Lord, her kindness and wisdom continue to light my way. Her recommendation wasn't just practical—it was a testament to the power of love and support during the hardest times.

Finding my fit was about more than just a prosthetic; it was about reclaiming a sense of self. While it didn't erase the scars or the loss, it gave me the confidence to move forward with dignity and strength.

Resilience and Hope

This journey taught me profound lessons about faith, resilience, and love. My scars remind me that life after cancer isn't just about survival—it's about living boldly and fully, embracing every moment with gratitude.

To anyone facing a recurrence or standing in front of their own mirror, I want you to know this: *You are more than your scars, and you are never alone.* With faith, love, and determination, there is always a way forward.

Through it all, I learned that faith doesn't erase the challenges but strengthens you to face them. I am here today, not just because of my fight, but because of God's grace, the love of those around me, and the resilience that grew in the face of adversity.

Just as challenges can recur, so can miracles.

Chapter 8

Chapter 8:
Divine Intervention: Blessings During the Battle

Baby Girl: Blessings During the Battle

Baby Girl. That's what I called the beautiful black SUV Ma had purchased specifically for my treatments in Durham. My nephew, Travis, found the perfect vehicle at his dealership, and Ma didn't hesitate—Travis delivered the vehicle, and Ma signed the papers. It wasn't just a car; it was a symbol of resilience during a time when so much felt uncertain. With its high ride and smooth drive, Baby Girl made every trip a little easier.

For a time, Ma and I swapped vehicles. She took my black Camry, complete with its sunroof, mounted telephone, and microphone near the sun visor, while I enjoyed the comfort and authority Baby Girl offered. Those little moments—her smiling as she explored the Camry's gadgets and me finding solace behind the wheel of the SUV—reminded us to find joy where we could, even in the midst of a storm.

An Unexpected Twist

One day, Ma called me at work, her voice filled with concern. *"The police are all around the house,"* she said. Baby Girl, parked in our driveway, had somehow become the subject of police interest. Our next-door neighbor, Mrs. Eva, had noticed the commotion and informed my Uncle Robert Lee, who happened to be in the neighborhood. He quickly jumped into action.

Uncle Robert Lee, always eager to lend a hand, stepped forward with what he believed was critical information. *"That SUV belongs to my niece,"* he began confidently. *"She's undergoing cancer treatments in Durham, and sometimes her friend Mary Frances drives her."* He paused, then added, as if to emphasize his point—or perhaps appear particularly insightful—Mary Frances's ethnicity.

What Uncle Robert Lee didn't realize was that his helpful explanation would ignite a *"gotcha"* moment for the detectives. Unbeknownst to him, the SUV in question matched the description of a vehicle linked to a jewelry store robbery in Chapel Hill. The suspects? Two women: one Black and one White.

Needless to say, Baby Girl was promptly impounded, caught in a web of circumstantial evidence before anyone could protest.

In his eagerness, Uncle Robert Lee also shared Ma's place of employment. Meanwhile, at Ma's job, the officers tracked her down. Never one to mince words, Ma later called me to recount the encounter, her voice brimming with indignation.

"I told them to get their 'ass' off my job!" she exclaimed. Then, with a mix of defiance and uncertainty, she added, *"I told them right, didn't I?"*

I wasn't sure whether to laugh or worry. *"Where are they now?"* I asked, my concern rising. After a moment's pause, I encouraged her, *"Meet me at the police station so we can get this straightened out."*

Although Ma had a kind and generous spirit, she had no problem setting the record straight when needed. She balanced her compassion with a quiet strength that let people know she meant business when the situation called for it.

Resolution Through Grace

At the police station, I recognized some of the detectives from my work over the years. They reviewed the evidence, and the mistake quickly became clear. Someone had transposed the numbers on the license tag. They matched Baby Girl's license plate, and a receipt that I had left in the truck from a local Hardee's, dated and time-stamped, proved it was impossible for the SUV to have been in Chapel Hill at the time of the robbery.

The next day, Baby Girl was released, and the ordeal was over. What could have been a distressing situation turned into a funny story we would laugh about for years. Uncle Robert Lee never missed a chance to retell his version of events, complete with dramatic flair, while Ma's resilience and humor continued to shine through.

After that incident, Mary Frances stopped transporting me. Officially, it was because her mother had fallen ill, and we certainly understood. Still, we often laugh about how she might have wanted to avoid Uncle Robert Lee—and any jewelry stores—just to be safe!

Our connection ran deep, bound not just by shared experiences but by a bond that felt like family—even if we didn't share the same DNA. Her unwavering spirit and steadfast support carried me thru some of my hardest days.

After one of my surgeries, Mary Frances had been present with the family, sitting in solidarity as they waited for updates.

When the nurse finally called and informed family members to go back to the recovery room, Mary Frances joined the group without hesitation. My brother James often tells the story of how the nurse stopped her, gently reminding her that only family was allowed beyond that point. Without skipping a beat, Mary Frances looked the nurse squarely in the eye and said firmly, "I am family." End of story. No further questions. Moments like these remind me of the true meaning of friendship and our true blood line connections. It knows no boundaries—neither distance nor ethnicity nor circumstance can diminish it. Friendship is the love we choose, the connections we honor, and the people who show up for us in the moments that matter most. And as for Baby Girl? She, too, remained steadfast, always ready for whatever came next.

Divine Intervention in the Parking Lot

Family and friends, with their good intentions, often seek to shield you from uncomfortable encounters. Yet one of the most profound blessings came from a chance encounter in a store parking lot.

Venturing to a local store with the intention of purchasing a lawnmower, I barely had the strength to walk in, let alone the funds to make a purchase or mow the lawn. Chemotherapy had drained me, both physically and financially. As I exited the store, weary and dispirited, I noticed a car parked beside mine. A lady inside struck up a conversation, her cheerful demeanor contrasting sharply with my inner turmoil.

Then, she asked, *"Girl, what did you do to your hair?* Her question caught me off guard, and I was initially hesitant to answer. I couldn't believe she would ask such a personal question. I proceeded to get into my vehicle, feeling a mix of emotions—anger, embarrassment, and sadness. But then, I felt convicted by the Holy Spirit. Something in her voice, or perhaps within myself, urged me to turn back and respond.

With a deep breath, I explained that I was undergoing chemotherapy, resulting in hair loss. As the words left my mouth, I braced myself for her reaction. To my surprise, her expression softened with empathy. This lady, who had always appeared perfectly put together with beautiful shoulder- length hair, reached her hand up and removed her wig to reveal her own struggle with a disease she called alopecia. Her vulnerability mirrored my own, creating an immediate bond between us. She shared that her husband had encouraged her to embrace her natural self, a step she had resisted for years. She expressed her intent to discuss this encounter with her husband that very day. We stood there in that parking lot, two women stripped of societal expectations, finding strength in our shared vulnerabilities.

Despite the paved parking lot, I am certain our excitement in leaving kicked up a bit of dirt. Divine intervention is amazing... and I thought I came to purchase a lawnmower.

This encounter gave me the extra strength and courage to walk in baldness with confidence. It reminded me that true beauty lies in our authenticity and our willingness to embrace our imperfections. To this day, that lady confidently rocks her bald head with beauty and grace, and I am forever grateful for the divine connection that empowered us both.

This is a tribute to Doris and Michael Perry. Michael has gone on to be with the Lord, but his spirit of kindness, strength, and encouragement continues to inspire us. His life was a testament to faith and perseverance, and the impact he had on both of us will never be forgotten. Doris, may you find comfort in knowing that his light still shines through the wisdom he shared and the lives he touched. We honor his memory today with gratitude and respect.

Mr. Right on Time: Love in Unexpected Places

As I faced cancer, one of the greatest blessings came in the form of love from an unexpected source. I call him Mr. Right on Time. We met just weeks before my initial diagnosis, and from the start, his presence felt like a gift from God. Where others might have been intimidated by my illness, he remained steadfast—a constant source of strength and support.

His love was tender yet strong, always encouraging me through the darkest days. What surprised me most was his ability to see beyond my illness. He never made me feel like a patient; instead, he treated me as a woman with dreams, hopes, and a future. His belief in me reignited my own hope and faith. His presence reminded me that love and grace often appear when we least expect them, and in the most beautiful ways.

Mr. Right on Time had a knack for bringing light into even the hardest moments. After difficult treatments, he would surprise me with cards, flowers, and even Blue's Clues balloons. These small gestures lifted my spirit in ways I didn't think possible.

He also offered practical support. When I decided to shave my head, he was right there, ready to guide me through the process. We had already discussed the effects of chemotherapy, so when my hair began to fall out, and he came prepared. He brought me a thoughtful kit containing everything I would need.

With gentle hands and a caring heart, he showed me step by step how to make the experience easier. He began by wetting my scalp with warm water, then carefully applied the shaving cream in even layers. With steady, deliberate strokes, he demonstrated how to use the razor to avoid nicks and irritation. Finally, he smoothed the moisturizing balm over my freshly shaved scalp to soothe and protect the skin, especially as stubble began to grow back. What could have been a painful and emotional moment was transformed into one of empowerment. His kindness and attention reminded me that even in moments of loss, there can be beauty in embracing change.

In every way, he was a beacon of light. His love was a constant reminder that, even in the hardest battles, beauty and blessings can emerge from the most unexpected places.

Mr. Right on Time reminded me that the greatest gifts in life often come disguised as the people who walk beside us, offering light and love when we need it most.

The Power of Love and Divine Guidance

My journey through cancer was undeniably difficult, but it was also filled with moments of grace and divine intervention. From Ma's steadfast love to an unexpected encounter in a parking lot, to the unwavering support of *Mr. Right on Time*, I was reminded that God's blessings often come when we need them most.

Through every twist and turn, I felt God's hand guiding me, reminding me that I was never alone.

Chapter 9

Chapter 9:
Juicing Through Adversity: Embracing Love & Support in My Breast Cancer Journey

The Port: A Lifeline for Many, But Not for Me

During chemotherapy treatments, many patients receive their medication through a port—an implanted device that allows for easier access to veins and reduces the discomfort of multiple needle pricks. It's considered the standard for chemotherapy administration, especially for stronger drugs like Adriamycin, affectionately known as the *"Red Devil"* due to its potent nature and striking red color. Yet, despite two separate diagnoses and rounds of chemotherapy, I never received a port. It's a rarity, and many consider it a blessing. Someone once told me, *"It's almost unheard of to go through chemotherapy without a port."* When I reflect on this, I realize my journey was, indeed, unique. Without a port, each treatment involved directly accessing my veins—each needle prick was a reminder of the strength I found within myself and the grace I received through faith.

Finding the Vein

I recall some days when finding a vein proved difficult. The nurses would wrap my arm in warm towels to help dilate the veins or encourage me to drink extra water before treatment, hoping to make the process easier. But no matter how prepared we were, there were still times when they struggled. I would silently pray, *God, please give them what they need every time they need it.* And almost as if in answer to my prayer, I'd hear the nurse say, *"We got it!"* Those words were music to my ears—an affirmation that, even in something as small as finding a vein, God was present and answering prayers.

The Red Devil

After a treatment of Adriamycin, fondly nicknamed the *"Red Devil"* for its striking red color, I became acquainted with its potent effects. Nurses donned protective gear when administering it intravenously, a testament to its strength not only in targeting cancer cells but also in harming healthy ones. Unfortunately, amidst its battle against cancer, it wreaked havoc on my body, leading to the development of mucositis and neuropathy. Despite the challenges, I sought solace in prayer, drawing strength from my faith in God.

Pastor Joann had given us sheets of scripture. We had scriptures taped on every mirror in the house and sheets in the car. We fervently prayed, clinging to the promises of God's word as our source of strength and comfort.

And through it all, I held onto the words of Isaiah 41:10: *"Fear not, for I am with you; be not dismayed, for I am your God; I will strengthen you, I will help you, I will uphold you with my righteous right hand."* These words became my anchor, reminding me that even in the darkest moments, I was not alone.

Chicken Love Soup

When I was too weak to lift my head, Ma's homemade chicken love soup became my sustenance. She spoon-fed me with such care, and each spoon was laced with a mother's love. We laughed about it later—I never stopped eating after that—but the truth was that the main ingredient wasn't chicken. It was her unwavering love.

Aunt Margaret and Juicing

Just when I thought I couldn't handle anything more, Aunt Margaret arrived—juicer in hand, determined to contribute to my recovery. My first thought? *Haven't I been through enough?* But Aunt Margaret, ever the innovator, pressed on. She had always been ahead of her time, finding unconventional ways to tackle life's challenges, and this time was no different.

As she bustled into the kitchen, I was flooded with memories of her unwavering presence in my life. Aunt Margaret had been a guiding light since childhood, always showing up exactly when I needed her. One memory, in particular, stood out—a day when trouble found me, and she became my savior.

I had defied my mother and ventured beyond the yard, something I knew was forbidden. But when I heard Ma's sharp call—"Ann!"—panic set in. Desperate to make it seem like I hadn't disobeyed, I bolted in the opposite direction, rounding the corner at full speed. That's when disaster struck.

I collided headfirst with a wrecked car in Ms. Shirley Mason's yard. Pain exploded through my leg. A jagged piece of the car's fender had torn into my flesh, and blood gushed from the wound. I could see the *white meat*, and fear gripped me—not just from the injury but from the certainty of my mother's wrath.

"Ann!" Ma's voice rang out again, her calls growing closer. My wails grew louder—not just from the pain, but from the trouble I knew was coming. Then, through my tears, I heard a different voice.

"What in the world?"

Aunt Margaret had stepped out onto her back porch. *Saved!* My escape route had always been through her yard. If I could make it seem like I had been there the whole time, maybe—just maybe—I wouldn't be in trouble.

I hobbled toward her, hollering dramatically, then collapsed into her arms. Aunt Margaret took one look at my injury and immediately took charge, her presence a shield of protection.

"She's alright, I got her," she reassured Ma, her calm tone dissolving the tension. As she tended to my wound, her touch carried the same warmth and care I would come to rely on throughout my life.

A Lifelong Anchor

Aunt Margaret's influence went far beyond moments like that. Years later, she taught me how to drive in her '62 Valiant, affectionately called the *Green Hornet*. The gear shift was on the collar, and despite my many scraped gears—and her occasional whiplash—she never once complained. The day I finally received my driver's permit was a joyful one for both of us. She had survived my learning phase, and I had gained a newfound sense of independence.

She was there for my greatest milestones—hosting my wedding celebration, offering wisdom through life's twists and turns. And when my marriage ended, she was there once again, not just with words of comfort but with action. In a show of solidarity, she enrolled in real estate school with me, walking beside me as I rebuilt my life from the ground up.

Aunt Margaret always showed up—with love, with wisdom, and sometimes, with grand ideas.

The Juicing Experiment

And now, she stood in my kitchen, excitement in her eyes and a state-of-the-art juicer that looked like it belonged in a science lab. She had done her research and was ready to make her case.

"This," she declared, placing a basket of vibrant fruits and deep green vegetables on the counter, "is the key to healing. Natural medicine."

I glanced at the produce and shook my head. I wasn't sold. Neither was Ma. We exchanged skeptical glances, silently agreeing—*this is too much.*

But Aunt Margaret wasn't one to give up easily. She switched tactics, her voice softening as she reached for my hand.

"Baby, I've loved you all your life," she said. "And cancer… it's taken too much from this family. But we are going to fight."

That was all it took. The air in the room shifted. Ma took my other hand. The sisters-in-love joined forces. Tears spilled, prayers lifted, and before I knew it, I was drinking the juice. (With a straw, of course.)

Reluctantly, I complied, sipping the bitter juice to make it somewhat bearable. Daily, I juiced, and before long, I noticed something. *The juice worked.* Slowly, I began to regain some energy. Ma tweaked Aunt Margaret's recipe to make it more palatable.

Soon, other cancer patients in the community heard about *Ms. Octavia's Juice*, and they came by to try it for themselves. The concoction became a symbol of hope.

And as they say, that's how the fight got started—against cancer, against fear, against anything that tried to take me down.

Aunt Margaret's vision, Ma's touch, and my faith turned a simple juice into something greater. It wasn't just about the ingredients; it was about the love poured into every glass, the strength behind every sip, and the community it built. What started as a juicing experiment became a testimony—a reminder that healing comes in many forms, but love is always the most powerful ingredient.

Chapter 10

Chapter 10:
A Mother's Sacrifice: Love, Loss and Legacy

After cancer ravaged my body, it turned its attention to my beloved mother. Her diagnosis in 2009 devastated us all, but in the five months that followed, we created some of the most precious memories of our lives.

For the first time as adults, my two brothers and I were home to live with Ma. Just the four of us under one roof, sharing love in ways we hadn't done since childhood. Despite her declining health, Ma continued to nurture us. I would leave "honey-do lists" for my brothers, only to return and find them unfinished. Ma and I would share quiet moments at night, laughing as she told me how my brothers would only spring into action when it was almost time for me to come home. Even through her illness, she found ways to make me laugh. She'd shake her head with a knowing grin, swearing me to secrecy about their lack of effort. Looking back, I realize Ma probably told them not to worry about the list. And the funny part? She likely swore them to secrecy as well. They must have known not to admit how little they'd done!

It makes me smile now, thinking about how she managed to keep the peace and shield us all from frustration, even in her illness. That's one of the things that made her sickness and loss so incredibly difficult. Ma had a way of making each of us feel special, as though we were the most important person in the world. Whether it was her children, grandchildren, siblings, nieces, nephews, or friends, she loved each of us with a personal and unique touch.

Sacrifice and Selflessness

Her treatment plan included oral chemotherapy. I will never forget the heartbreak of having to administer those pills, knowing the toll they would take on her body. Each time I handed her those pills, I knew the nausea and sickness that would follow. Yet, she endured it without complaint, out of love for us. I pleaded with her to drink the juice that Aunt Margaret and she had insisted I drink during my treatments—an awful concoction that, although effective, was hard to swallow. But Ma, ever the mother, refused to take it herself. Mothers pull rank like that.

One day, as we sat together on the front porch, Ma made a declaration that shook me to my core: "I'm not going to take any more treatments." My heart stopped. I wanted to scream, to beg her not to give up. But instead, I whispered a prayer and asked God for the right words. Desperation threatened to consume me, but I remembered the teachings of Mrs. Walker, my former supervisor, who always told me to give people "getting up room"—to respect their space to make decisions. I remembered a conversation we had months earlier when I had expressed concern about her weight loss. In her vulnerability, she felt hurt, thinking I was saying she looked bad. I apologized that evening, promising never to bring it up again.

Instead of arguing or pleading, I simply asked, "Ma, why did you start taking the treatment in the first place?"

Her response pierced my heart: "I did it for y'all."

Her words shattered me. She had been enduring the painful effects of chemotherapy for our sake, not hers. She had been suffering, willingly, to ease our hearts. To give us peace of mind that she had tried everything, so we would never feel like she had given up. Even in her final moments, she was thinking of us, not herself. Her love was unselfish, unwavering, and without limits.

Tears welled up in my heart. I couldn't let her see them, though. I had to respect her decision, even as the knowledge of what it meant tore me apart. How do you argue with someone who has already sacrificed so much? How do you tell your mother, who has spent her entire life putting others first, that her choice is too hard for you to accept?

Her strength wasn't just in enduring the treatments—it was in why she endured them. Even as her body weakened, her love for us remained unshakable. She carried the weight of our feelings, our fears, and our hopes on her shoulders, never letting us see how heavy the burden truly was.

Living Through the Pain

Even before Ma received her diagnosis, I sensed something was wrong. Despite her illness, she was determined to care for me. When we moved into our new home next door, we didn't even need a moving company; we literally walked our belongings across the yard. Ma surprised me with a dining room set, a gesture of her endless generosity. But soon, exhaustion took over, and days later, we both ended up in the emergency room.

Separated in the ER, Ma never disclosed her diagnosis to me. It was her way of protecting me, just as she had always done. I was struggling with the effects of mucositis from pushing my chemo treatments, and I wanted to focus on caring for her. But she bore her pain quietly, never wanting to burden anyone with the truth of how much she endured.

Her strength and resilience astounded me. Even as cancer weakened her body, her spirit remained strong. She continued to work, even at 78 years old, driving fifteen minutes on her lunch break to prepare food for me. If she couldn't make it, she'd ensure someone else, like "Reverend Perry," was there to care for me. Her love knew no bounds.

A Final Declaration of Love

In April 2009, we took a family trip to Georgia with my brother James, his wife Rosa, and Ma's best friend, Aunt Bett. It was during that trip that Ma could no longer conceal her illness. Upon returning to North Carolina, our first stop was at Ma's doctor's office. After extensive testing, we learned the devastating news: Ma had cancer.

Her fight with cancer was brief, and by September of 2009, just fourteen months after moving into our new house, Ma passed away.

In her final days and after, I struggled with guilt, feeling as though she had sacrificed too much for me. Aunt Belle would call to check on me, always asking the same question: "Shug, do you have anything you want to tell me?" For the longest time, I held back. But one day, I broke down and told her everything. Her response was simple but profound: "Shug, that's what mothers do. That was a mother's love." She chose to sacrifice, not out of obligations, but of an unshakable love. Aunt Belle set me free.

A Legacy of Love

Ma's love and sacrifice were a reflection of the love I needed to extend to myself. It took me a long time to let go of the guilt, but eventually, I realized that the best way to honor Ma's legacy was to love myself as unconditionally as she had loved me.

Her life was a testament to the power of love, sacrifice, and grace. Her love for each of us was undeniable and deeply personal. It didn't matter if you were a child, grandchild, family or friend. She always knew exactly what we needed- whether it was encouragement, a gentle nudge in the right direction, a few dollars given in secret or even correction when necessary. She wasn't just the cheerleader, she was the entire squad, lifting you up but keeping you accountable. When I think about the sacrifices, I strive to do my best—embracing life with the same open heart she did.

If you are walking through grief, know this—you are not alone. Families struggle, they break, they hurt—but love does not die.

Give yourself and others grace. The love that held you together before loss is still there. And the best way to honor those we've lost is to keep loving the ones who are still here.

Chapter 11

Chapter 11:
No Pockets:
Identifying a Patient Need

Imagine standing in a department store, surrounded by rows of bras in every size, color, and style imaginable. Yet, despite the array of options, none seem to cater to your unique needs. You sift through rack after rack, feeling the weight of frustration mounting with each fruitless search. It's a feeling that sinks deep into my soul during this journey—a journey marked by resilience, frustration, and ultimately, empowerment. Trying to find a bra becomes a challenge, testing my patience and resolve.

From a young age, we're taught that a bra is more than just a piece of clothing; it's a symbol of femininity and identity. However, this perception often clashes with the reality many women encounter, especially those who undergo mastectomy surgery. As a plus-size mastectomy cancer survivor, the journey of finding beautiful and sexy bras after my surgery in 2008 was vastly different from the expectations ingrained in me since childhood. Instead of feeling empowered, I faced an exhausting and frustrating challenge.

As someone who has always valued style and self-expression, the inability to find bras that made me feel like myself was a blow to my confidence. I struggled with body image issues and feelings of inadequacy, wondering if I would ever reclaim my sense of femininity and beauty. After years of searching for that elusive, beautiful fuchsia bra, it dawned on me: the market lacked thoughtfully designed mastectomy bras that truly catered to both function and fashion. It became painfully clear that this status quo wasn't going to change.

Breaking Barriers

The frustration of not finding bras that accommodated my needs—whether it was pockets for my prosthesis, tailoring a standard bra, or being told by a department store that mastectomy bras were not worth selling—only fueled my determination. I vividly recall days spent hopping from store to store, searching for a bra that blended functionality with style, only to feel disappointed time and time again. The frustration reached its peak, and I took matters into my own hands. I purchased fabrics and enrolled in a bra-making class to learn about the process. Eventually, I commissioned a seamstress to custom make a bra for me. Then, COVID-19 changed the world—but not my need.

This challenge, faced as a plus-size woman and breast cancer survivor, prompted me to write *Loving Me*. It's not just a book sharing my story—it sheds light on the struggles that countless women silently endure, battling to find lingerie that makes them feel confident and comfortable.

I aim to inspire and empower other women facing similar challenges. I want them to know they are not alone, their experiences are valid, and there is strength in sharing our stories. Together, let's ignite conversations about body positivity, inclusivity, and the need for representation in fashion and beauty. Every woman deserves to feel confident and empowered in her own skin, regardless of her medical history.

Beauty, Dignity, and the Search for Confidence

I walked into a store, heart full of hope, only to leave 50 miles later in tears. I wasn't just searching for a bra—I was searching for dignity.

After my mastectomy, bra shopping transformed from a fun outing into an exhausting and often humiliating ordeal. At home, my drawer held colorful reminders of how things were before—leopard print, lace, and frills that once made me feel confident and beautiful. Running my fingers over the fabrics, I sighed. Did I take it all for granted?

Determined to find something that fit, I scheduled an appointment at a store where a sales associate assured me that they could accommodate my needs. My heart lifted as I spotted a vibrant display of colorful bras—bright reds, soft pinks, deep purples, and playful leopard prints. For a moment, I imagined myself wearing them—feeling confident, vibrant, and like myself again. Could this be it?

Excitement bubbled as I reminded the associate of our appointment. With a polite smile, I joked, "I'll take them all!" She hesitated before responding, "Ma'am, the plus-size mastectomy bras are in the back."

My heart sank. The salesclerk, like many people, sometimes used terms that can be offensive, even if unintentionally. "Normal" bras for "normal" women. "Special needs." The words stung, making me feel excluded — as though my journey placed me outside what was considered normal. I wished she had been trained to use inclusive language—to acknowledge that I had specific needs without implying I didn't belong. When she returned, the bras she brought were beige, lifeless, and devoid of lace or color. Functional, yes, but uninspiring.

Worse, none seemed designed to accommodate my prosthesis comfortably. They looked nothing like the vibrant bras I had seen on display.

I asked why the plus-size bras were hidden in the back. She mumbled something about "insurance purposes," but I believed the truth was that plus-size mastectomy bras were treated as an afterthought, hidden from view to avoid discomforting others. The absurdity struck me. If these bras were kept out of sight for "insurance purposes," wouldn't they be displayed under reinforced glass, like designer bags? Why should survivors, already grappling with so much, be made to feel like their needs are less deserving of beauty and celebration?

Sparking Change

On the drive home, I cried. I thought of the survivors like me that face similar situations. That experience fueled my determination to create change.

Society's fixation on a narrow standard of beauty often leaves anyone who doesn't fit the mold feeling excluded. Plus-size women, especially those who've had mastectomies, are doubly marginalized. This isn't just about lingerie; it's about inclusivity, representation, and honoring the individuality of every woman. It's also about education—training store associates to use empowering, inclusive language so that no woman ever feels diminished by a single word.

I wanted to tell survivors that life after surgery is about more than survival—it's about reclaiming joy and confidence. Shopping for lingerie should never make a woman feel ashamed or overlooked. Every woman deserves the dignity of choices that reflect her individuality and celebrate her strength.

That's how *Loving Me* was born. It wasn't just about bras. It was about addressing the gap in representation, challenging outdated norms, and building a future where survivors feel seen and valued. My hope is that *Loving Me* sparks change—encouraging the fashion industry to embrace all women, regardless of size or medical history, and reminding every survivor that she is beautiful, whole, and deserving of celebration.

Jeremiah 29:11 remains my guiding scripture: *"For I know the plans I have for you," declares the Lord, "plans to prosper you and not to harm you, plans to give you hope and a future."*

Chapter 12

Chapter 12:
Naked:
Finding Purpose in the Pain

W hen I first heard the words *"breast cancer,"* it felt like my world shattered. I had just come out of a seventeen-year marriage, bruised and battered from a painful divorce. I thought I had faced the worst of it, but life had other plans. Another battle loomed—one I wasn't sure I had the strength to fight. I didn't want to deal with it. I was angry—so angry. I kept asking, *"Why me?"* as if somewhere, somehow, there was an answer that could make sense of it all. But there was only silence.

The nights were the hardest. Lying alone in bed, the tears would come, unstoppable. Fear would grip me in those dark, quiet moments, and it felt like I was suffocating under the weight of my own uncertainty. The questions never stopped spinning in my mind: *Will I survive this? Can we change this somehow? What will happen to my family? How much more can I take?* I never thought I was going to die—it wasn't that. I feared how much more I could endure.

Desperate for relief, I turned to prayer. Every night, I poured my heart out to God. I wasn't asking for a miracle—I just wanted to know *why*. I begged for guidance, for clarity, for anything that would give me a sense of direction. But for weeks, there was nothing but the sound of my own quiet sobs.

And then, one night, something shifted. It wasn't a voice or a vision, but a quiet peace began to settle over me, like a gentle breeze in the middle of a storm. It felt like a weight had been lifted. In that moment, I whispered the question that had been burning in my soul: *"God, what do you want me to do with this?"*

It wasn't an instant transformation. The next steps were slow and painful. I confided in Pastor Joann, who became my lifeline. Pastor Joann didn't offer easy solutions. She spoke with the kind of wisdom that only comes from walking through fire herself. *"You have to forgive,"* she told me. *"Not just your ex-husband, but yourself. Let go of the anger, or it will destroy you before the cancer ever gets the chance."* She also encouraged me to surround myself with positive people.

So, I began the painful process of forgiveness. I forgave my ex-husband for the hurt, the broken promises, and everything that had led to the end of our marriage. But more importantly, I forgave myself. I let go of the shame and the guilt. When people asked what had happened between us, I no longer gave long-winded explanations. I simply said, *"We failed to work out our differences."* It was the truth, stripped of blame or bitterness, and that truth set me free.

Slowly, the fog began to lift. I realized that this journey wasn't just about surviving cancer—it was about finding a new purpose in the chaos. I clung to a verse from the Bible, *Jeremiah 29:11*: *"For I know the plans I have for you,"* declares the Lord, *"plans to prosper you and not to harm you, plans to give you hope and a future."*

Those words became my lifeline. They reminded me that my story wasn't over. There was a plan for me, even if I couldn't see it in the midst of the storm. And so, I kept moving forward—one painful, determined step at a time.

As the days turned into weeks and the weeks into months, I began to embrace the journey. My pain became my purpose. Every scar, every tear, every sleepless night became a part of a story that wasn't just mine to carry—it was meant to be shared. I realized that my battle wasn't just about me. My story could be a light for others walking through their own darkness.

Cancer took so much from me, but it gave me something, too—a strength I never knew I had. It taught me that even in the darkest moments, there's a glimmer of hope. Even when it feels like everything is falling apart, there's a reason to keep fighting. And that reason? It's not just to survive. It's to *live*—to live fully, boldly, and with purpose.

I've learned that sometimes the most beautiful things are born from the most painful places. And this battle, as brutal as it was, gave me the gift of clarity. I found my strength. I found my voice. And I found that, even in the midst of brokenness, there is always light to be found.

This chapter of my life wasn't just about surviving cancer. It was about being *transformed* by it. I was stripped bare—naked in my vulnerability—but in that space, I discovered who I truly was. Cancer didn't define me, but it did refine me.

In those quiet moments, when the world felt heavy and the tears flowed freely, I learned the most important lesson of all: my pain had purpose. And that purpose was far greater than I could have ever imagined.

If you're reading this and you feel broken, if you feel lost in your own storm, know this—there's still light ahead. There's still a plan. There's still hope. Hold on, keep fighting, and trust that one day, the pain you're walking through will reveal a purpose you never expected.

This isn't just my story—it's our story. And together, we'll keep walking forward, finding purpose in every scar, every tear, and every moment we choose to rise again.

Chapter 13

Chapter 13:
Parallel Paths
Stories of Strength & Resilience

Walking Through Their Battles

In my journey with breast cancer, I encountered countless souls fighting their own battles in silence, carrying burdens heavier than words could ever convey. Each story is a thread in the tapestry of resilience, woven together by courage, faith, and an unbreakable spirit. In this chapter, we walk alongside three remarkable women—**Andrea, Linda, and Ms. Deborah**—each offering a unique perspective on the complexities of breast cancer and the indomitable strength that connects us all.

Andrea's Journey: The Silent Battle

Andrea's battle with breast cancer was marked by quiet courage. She faced her diagnosis with grace and strength, embodying the power of hope even in the darkest moments.

One night in 2001, after a family reunion, I received a call from my cousin Andrea—whom we all affectionately called Niecy. My head was bald, my spirit weary from the relentless cycle of chemotherapy and doctor visits. Despite the exhaustion weighing me down, I welcomed her when she asked if she could stop by my house.

Andrea carried with her a stillness, a calm presence that belied the storm inside her. She had seen me at my most vulnerable, my battle laid bare before family. Yet, as we sat together in the quiet of my home, she finally voiced the question that had been pressing on her heart.

"How do you handle it?" she asked softly, her eyes filled with uncertainty and quiet desperation.

I offered her what comfort I could, sharing the lessons I had learned in my fight. But there was something in her voice, something in the way she asked, that lingered with me long after she left.

It wasn't until later that I learned the truth—Andrea had been fighting her own battle with breast cancer, silently. She had waged a war she never asked for. Andrea chose to keep her diagnosis private. In the end, she confided in her brother during her final days, before she succumbed to the disease.

Andrea's story is a heartbreaking reminder of the silent battles so many fight, often hidden beneath layers of strength. She never shared the full extent of her journey with me, but her quiet courage left an indelible mark on my heart. She taught me that even in the face of unbearable pain, there is grace.

As I carry her memory, I am reminded of the profound interconnectedness of our shared struggles—the bonds that unite us, the hardships that shape us, and the legacy of resilience that lives on long after we are gone.

Scripture Reflection

"Carry each other's burdens, and in this way, you will fulfill the law of Christ." — Galatians 6:2

Linda's Journey: Reclaiming Femininity

Linda's journey through breast cancer left a lasting mark on me—a testament to grace, generosity, and the quiet courage that shines even in the darkest times. Through her battle, Linda's warmth remained, illuminating the lives of everyone around her, even as she wrestled with her own fears.

For months after her surgery, Linda hid beneath oversized shirts, using layers of fabric to conceal the scars that had forever altered her body. She carried the weight of shame and insecurity, afraid of how the world might judge her. The external world, however, had moved on, offering solutions and support Linda never knew existed. While the *Women's Health and Cancer Rights Act* had made prosthetics more accessible, Linda wasn't initially aware of these options—and when she learned about them, she decided that prosthetics were not the best fit for her. Instead, she chose to embrace a *flat closure*, a decision as unique and personal as her journey.

One day, in the quiet space of my office, she finally opened up. Tears welled in her eyes as she shared her fears—the struggle to reclaim her femininity, the fear of judgment, and the longing to feel whole again.

In that vulnerable moment, I felt compelled to share my own journey with her. I talked about my mastectomy—the fear, the uncertainty, and the long road to self-acceptance. I told her how I had learned to embrace my body and my scars, reclaiming both my sense of self and my womanhood.

Linda listened closely; her eyes wide with recognition. She realized she wasn't alone. In me, she saw a fellow warrior, someone who had walked the path she was just beginning to navigate. And with that knowledge, she found the strength to begin her own healing process.

Choosing to honor her decision to forgo prosthetics, Linda embraced her flat closure with courage and determination. The road was not easy. There were moments of doubt and discomfort. But slowly, Linda began to blossom, reclaiming her sense of femininity in a way that felt authentic and true to her. She emerged from the shadows stronger and more confident than ever before.

Watching her transformation, I was reminded that true beauty is not found in perfection. It's found in the courage to embrace our imperfections, to love ourselves fiercely, and to face the world as we are—scars and all.

Ms. Deborah's Journey: A Legacy of Grace

Ms. Deborah's journey with terminal cancer left an indelible mark on my heart. Though our battles were different, her strength, love, and unwavering spirit became a beacon of inspiration for me. Even now, her legacy continues to shape my mission to bring light to others.

The turning point came during a visit arranged by Pastor Clayton. His trust in me to join him on this deeply personal trip touched me profoundly. He introduced me to Ms. Deborah, his dear friend, and in doing so, entrusted me with a sacred moment of witnessing her grace in the midst of suffering.

We traveled down east, carrying a small gift—lemon drops, affectionately referred to by Pastor Clayton as *"rock candy."* It was a simple offering, yet when we presented it to Ms. Deborah, her face lit up with gratitude and warmth. Despite her own pain, she welcomed us with grace that left a lasting impression. That visit changed me forever.

Pastor Clayton's trust in me was humbling and transformative. In including me in such a sacred moment, he showed confidence in my ability to not only witness her light but to carry it forward. That experience awakened in me a deeper sense of purpose—a calling to offer hope and encouragement to others, just as Ms. Deborah had done for us that day.

Ms. Deborah taught me that even when cancer takes our bodies, it cannot diminish the light of our spirit. Her life was a testimony of faith, strength, and love, and she showed me that the greatest gift we can offer one another is hope. Her legacy fuels my desire to serve, to share light with those in their darkest moments, and to honor her witness of grace.

As Pastor Clayton would say, "Holy Spirit my sweet constant companion." And in that moment, I knew Jesus was there. God has been my sweet constant companion. He was there that day, holding us all in His hands. I am forever grateful for the impact Ms. Deborah had on my journey and for the trust Pastor Clayton placed in me to carry her light forward.

These women—**Andrea, Linda, and Ms. Deborah**—each taught me something invaluable about strength, resilience, and the power of the human spirit. Their stories are woven into my own journey, and they remind me daily that even in the midst of suffering, there is beauty, there is hope, and there is always a reason to keep fighting.

Their lives have become part of my mission, my purpose, and my testimony. They remind me that love, courage, and grace are not just words—they are guiding lights that can carry us through even the darkest of battles.

Chapter 14

Chapter 14:
The Blessings Through the Storm

November 11, 2020: A Journey with Jesus

Now, back to my story…

As I sat in the waiting room at Duke Medical Center everything felt different that morning. For the first time in 19 years, I attended my routine mammogram appointment alone. No physical companion sat beside me, no hand to hold as I waited for results.

For nearly two decades, God had blessed me with someone by my side for every single appointment. Rain or shine, through sickness and health, He had encamped His angels around me. My mother used to ask me whenever I left the house, "Who's going with you?" My answer was always the same: "Jesus and me." Today, that simple statement was my reality. It was just Jesus and me.

The world had changed. The shadow of COVID-19 hung over everything, transforming routines, isolating people, and redefining what companionship looked like. Where waiting rooms had once been full of quiet murmurs, whispered prayers, and the nervous tapping of fingers on armrests, they now felt empty and eerily silent. Chairs sat spaced apart, signs reminded everyone to keep their distance, and masks hid the expressions that once offered comfort. But through it all, one thing remained constant: Jesus was still with me.

An Unexpected Turn

The day before had started like any other mammogram appointment. I went through the familiar steps: changing into a gown, standing for the imaging, and waiting in the sterile room for the results. But when the door to the left opened, and my name was called.

My heart dropped! The mammogram had detected something.

In the ultrasound room, the doctor pointed to the screen, showing me the dark oval-shaped mass—about half a centimeter long. He tried to reassure me, saying that its small size was a positive sign.

But size didn't matter to me. A knot formed in my stomach, tightening with every word he spoke. A biopsy was recommended—immediately.
I wasn't ready. My phone buzzed with messages from concerned family and friends, but I couldn't respond. I needed time—to pray, to breathe, to process.

How did such a clear November morning turn gray so suddenly? I thought back to my drive to the hospital earlier that day. The sky had been so blue, the air so crisp, and I had felt free—celebrating nearly 12 years cancer-free since my last diagnosis in 2008.

But now, a dark mass stared back at me from the ultrasound screen.

Jesus and Me

That evening, I spoke with my family. I could hear the worry in their voices, but I assured them that the doctor had promised everything would be fine. I scheduled my biopsy for the next morning at 8:30 a.m.

When asked who would accompany me, I gave them the same answer: "Jesus and Me." Above all, I knew I needed to face this appointment alone.

I gathered my prayer warriors. They all offered to drive me, to sit with me, to wait for me. But I declined. This was my journey—mine and Jesus'.

"Just Jesus and me," I said.

The Biopsy

The next morning, I walked into the clinic alone, signed in, and took my seat. A new care team greeted me, unfamiliar faces from the day before.

My assigned doctor introduced herself as Dr. Peacock. I nearly laughed out loud. One of my friends is a gospel comedian, and her stage name is Mrs. Peacock. I shared the story with Dr. Peacock, and we both chuckled at God's undeniable sense of humor.

Dr. Peacock explained the procedure in detail. They would start with a needle aspiration. If the mass was a cyst, the needle would resolve it on the spot, and no biopsy would be needed. But if the mass persisted, they would proceed with a biopsy.

She spoke gently explaining what would happen if the results were benign—or if they were malignant. I nodded along, though her words felt like a faint echo in my mind. I'd heard them all before.

As they prepped me for the needle aspiration, they struggled to locate the mass. My heart raced. Did I even want them to find it? But it was too late—the needle found its target.

A moment later, I heard Dr. Peacock say the words that felt like a breath of fresh air: *"It's resolved."*

Could it be? Just like that? Relief washed over me in waves. *"Thank you, Jesus. Thank you."*

No signs of malignancy. I was instructed to return in one year for a follow-up mammogram.

The Drive Home

I drove home with the windows partially rolled down despite the November chill. The fresh air filled my lungs, and for the first time in hours, I felt like I could breathe again.

I thought back to the left door of the waiting room—the door that had opened so many times over the years. Looking back, I see now that those doors weren't just entrances to tests or diagnoses. They were doorways to deeper faith, resilience, and gratitude.

Over the years, cancer has taught me many things. It's shown me the power of faith, the importance of family, friends and the quiet strength that lives within all of us. Most importantly, it's reminded me that every battle, every scar, and every tear is woven into a story far greater than I could ever imagine. I walked into that clinic alone, but I was never truly alone.

It was always Jesus and me. Jeremiah 29:11

A Letter to Myself

In the quiet moments that followed, I sat down to reflect on this journey—the fear, the hope, the unwavering presence of Jesus beside me.

I decided to write a letter to myself—a tangible reminder of this moment, of the triumph, of God's faithfulness.

Dear Freddie,

I just want to take a moment to tell you how proud I am of you. You've been through so much, yet you've kept pushing forward with strength, courage, and faith. No matter what life has thrown your way, you've stood tall and kept going, even when the road was rough.

Your scars tell a story—not of defeat, but of survival, resilience, and grace. You've turned pain into power, fear into faith, and doubt into determination. And through it all, you've never lost sight of the truth: God's got you.

As you step into this next chapter, remember this—you are enough, just as you are. Celebrate your wins, big or small. Embrace every part of yourself, flaws and all. Love yourself the way you love others—fully, fiercely, and without hesitation.

Taking care of yourself isn't selfish—it's necessary. Keep giving yourself grace. Keep leaning into the love and light that surrounds you. And never forget: The price has already been paid! You are worthy of every bit of joy coming your way.

Hold this letter close as a reminder of who you are and how far you've come. Keep soaring, Freddie—the best is yet to come.

With love and admiration,
Me

Nuggets to Take Away from My Journey...

- [ ] Your voice matters in the doctor's office. Ask questions, seek second opinions, and advocate for the care you deserve. Your health is too important to stay silent—be your own best advocate.

- [ ] Healing is not just physical—it's emotional and spiritual too. Give yourself permission to grieve, to rest, and to grow. True healing happens when you nurture not just your body, but also your mind and soul.

- [ ] As we gather for family reunions, birthdays, and family gatherings to celebrate our shared history, let's also take a moment to talk about our health. Knowledge is power, and understanding our family's medical past can help us make informed decisions for a healthier future.

- [ ] Breast cancer awareness isn't just for October—it's for every day. A diagnosis can come at any time, and early detection saves lives. Don't miss your scheduled mammograms. Let's commit to year-round awareness, education, and support, because every day is the right day to prioritize our health.

- [ ] A diagnosis can be overwhelming, and sometimes, you just can't find the words to share. It's not about shutting people out—it's about processing, healing, and surviving. Support isn't always in conversation; sometimes, it's in silent understanding, presence, and love.

A Closing Message of Hope

There was a time when life shifted in ways I never expected. Some days were heavy—filled with uncertainty, loss, and the weight of the unknown. But even in those moments, something greater was at work. I was being refined, strengthened, and prepared for something beyond my understanding.

I remember standing in front of the mirror, staring at a reflection I barely recognized. My hair was gone. My body had changed. And for a moment, I wondered, *who am I?* But then, something shifted. I stopped focusing on what was missing and began to see what remained—my strength, my spirit, my will to keep loving myself through it all.

I may have lost a part of me, but I gained something greater—resilience, love, and the courage to embrace myself fully.

And so, to you, my dear reader, I offer this:

No matter what season of life you are in, take a moment to remind yourself:

I am worthy of joy. I am worthy of love. I am worthy of living fully.

Say it. Believe it. Walk in that truth.

This book is more than my journey—it is an invitation to healing, strength, and self-love. If my story has touched you, let it be a spark in your own life. Share your truth.

Lift someone up. Remind another soul that they, too, are worthy of joy, love, and a life fully lived.

As you turn this final page, may you step forward with courage, knowing your story is still being written. You are here. You are loved. And you are enough.

Through every step of my journey, the hand of God, my family, and my friends have upheld me. I pray that same love and strength surround you as you move forward.

A Prayer for You

Lord,

For every person reading this, may they be reminded of their worth, their strength, and the beauty of who they are. Let them know they are never alone—that You are with them, holding them up through every season of life. Cover them with Your peace, courage, and unshakable hope.

I lift up the women on this journey—those fighting, those healing, and those walking forward in strength. May they know they are fearfully and wonderfully made. Surround them with love, and remind them that even in their hardest moments, they are never alone.

And Lord, I lift up the caregivers—the ones who stand beside, comfort, and carry the weight of love and support. Give them endurance, wisdom, and rest, and remind them that their labor is not in vain.

Whatever challenges they may face, may they find peace, courage, and healing in Your unfailing love.

Amen.

RESOURCES

Breast Cancer
https://www.cancer.org/cancer/types/breast-cancer.html

Living as a Breast Cancer Survivor
https://www.cancer.org/cancer/types/breast-cancer/living-as-a-breast-cancer-survivor.html

The Americans with Disabilities Act (ADA):
https://www.ada.gov/

Americans With Disabilities Act: Information for People Facing Cancer
https://www.cancer.org/cancer/financial-insurance-matters/health-insurance-laws/americans-with-disabilities-act.html

Breast Reconstruction Surgery
https://www.cancer.org/cancer/types/breast-cancer/reconstruction-surgery.html

No matter where you are in this journey, know that every stage has purpose, every challenge is shaping you, and you are emerging into the incredible, unstoppable woman you were always meant to be.

~Freddie Harris

It's Okay—Say My Name

In Loving Memory of My Niece, Rhonda Howard

Rhonda Howard enjoyed life. She was loving, fun, and had a heart that knew no limits. She would literally give you the shirt off her back—because that's who she was. She cared deeply, always willing to give her last to help someone else.

Even in the midst of her own pain, she remained an encourager—lifting others up, reminding them to keep going, and offering strength when she had every reason to seek it for herself. Her kindness and generosity touched everyone who knew her. She was a warrior, a light, and a voice that should never be forgotten.

Her journey with breast cancer was not just her own—it was a call to action for all of us. Breast cancer awareness is more than a conversation; it is a responsibility. It means knowing our risks, advocating for our health, and ensuring that no one walks this path alone.

To my nephews and nieces:

Let Rhonda's story remind you that your health is your power.

- Get your annual exams—breast cancer doesn't wait. Early detection saves lives.
- Make sure your care team not just listens but truly hears you. Your voice matters.

- ☐ Know your family history—and make sure your doctors know it too. When they ask, **It's OK—Say My Name**. Family history can shape your care and save your life.
- ☐ Advocate for yourself and others. No one should walk this journey alone.

We honor Rhonda by making sure her story is not lost—by taking action, by making informed health choices, and by speaking up.

It's Okay—Say My Name.

Say it when you talk to your doctor.
Say it when you share your family history.
Say it for those we've lost.
Say it for those still fighting.
Say it because knowledge saves lives.

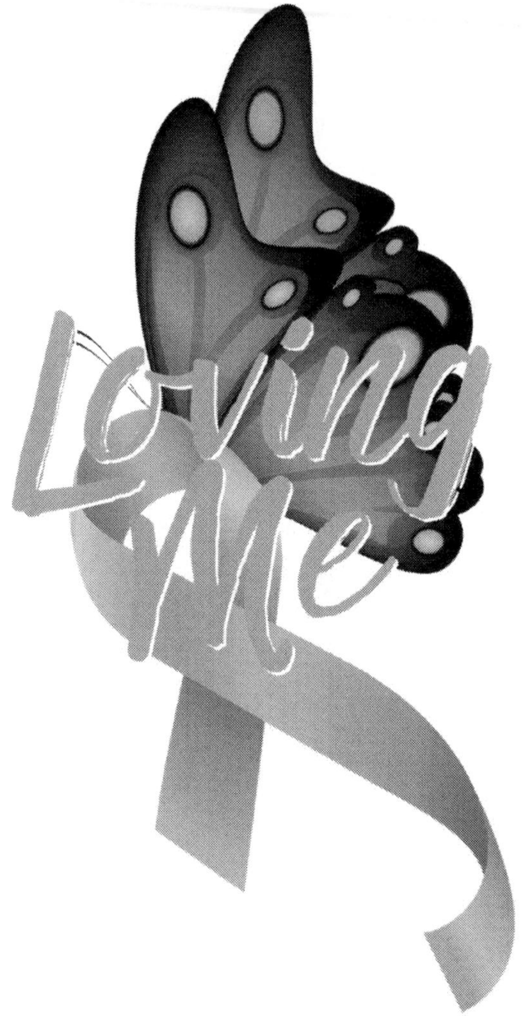
Loving Me

ABOUT THE LOGO
The Journey of a Butterfly

The logo for **Loving Me LLC** is more than just an image—it represents the transformation every breast cancer warrior undergoes. Just as a butterfly moves through stages of change, so too does a woman navigating this journey. It's not just about survival; it's about resilience, renewal, and stepping into a new kind of strength.

1. **The Egg (Diagnosis & Uncertainty)**
   The moment of diagnosis feels like being frozen in place, unsure of what's ahead. It is a time of fear, questions, and uncertainty. Just like the egg holds the potential for new life, this stage holds the weight of what's to come—the first step into a journey of strength.

2. **The Caterpillar (Treatment & Endurance)**
   The caterpillar's job is to grow, to push forward despite challenges, much like a woman undergoing treatment. The days feel long, the changes feel overwhelming, and yet, through it all, she moves forward. There is exhaustion, but also resilience. She learns to adapt, to fight, to survive.

3. **The Chrysalis (Healing & Transformation)**
   The cocoon is where the deepest transformation happens, hidden from the world. This is the stage of healing, physically and emotionally. It is a time of uncertainty, self-reflection, and faith. Though the struggle is unseen, change is happening. A new version of herself is forming.

4. **The Butterfly (Remission, Renewal & Empowerment)**
And then, one day, she emerges—not the same as before, but beautifully transformed. She carries the scars of her journey, but they do not define her; they empower her. The butterfly represents the survivor—stronger, wiser, and more radiant. She no longer just survives—she thrives.

MY CANCER JOURNEY OF RESILIENCE & SELF-LOVE

Loving Me

FREDDIE HARRIS

About The Author
AUTHOR FREDDIE HARRIS

About The Author
AUTHOR FREDDIE HARRIS

A Survivor, Advocate, and Beacon of Hope

Freddie Harris is a shining example of resilience, faith, and purpose-driven living. Twice she faced the devastating storm of breast cancer, and twice she emerged stronger, carrying with her a story not just of survival but of transformation, hope, and unwavering faith in God's plan.

Her journey has been marked by profound loss, including the passing of her beloved mother, yet through it all, Freddie discovered her true calling: to inspire, empower, and advocate for women navigating their own cancer battles. She turned her pain into purpose, using her voice to uplift others and ensure no woman feels unseen or unsupported on her journey.

Recognizing the emotional and physical struggles women face after mastectomy surgery, Freddie was inspired to explore the creation of mastectomy bras designed for plus-size women—lingerie that would offer both comfort and confidence while celebrating femininity. Although that vision didn't materialize as planned, it led to something even greater: **Loving Me LLC,** a brand that embodies self-love, resilience, and the beauty of survivorship. It also became the foundation for her book,

Loving Me, where she shares her raw and heartfelt journey –filled with loss, triumph, and unyielding faith.

The book is more than just a memoir, it's a guide, a source of strength, and a call to embrace life with courage and love. Through her words, Freddie reminds readers that scars tell stories, faith moves mountains, and even in the darkest storms, light can break through.

As Freddie connected with more survivors, she realized that healing is about more than just what you wear—it's about community, shared experiences, and having a support system. This realization sparked the creation of *S!sters Speak L!fe*, a nonprofit dedicated to empowering breast cancer survivors through education, advocacy, and encouragement.

Through *S!sters Speak L!fe*, Freddie has created a powerful space where survivors find strength, share their stories, and access vital resources to help them thrive. One of the signature initiatives is the annual 3D mammography screening event, which brings mobile screenings directly to the community, reinforcing the message that early detection saves lives. Freddie's work continues to uplift and inspire, reminding women that survivorship isn't just about overcoming—it's about fully embracing life.

Beyond her advocacy work, Freddie is a retired social worker, proud member of the National Association of Realtors and a licensed Real Estate Broker with Coldwell Banker Advantage. Whether serving her clients in real estate or leading her mission-driven initiatives, Freddie approaches every role with integrity, compassion, and a deep commitment to making a difference.

Freddie Harris is more than a survivor—she is a voice for the voiceless, a champion for the forgotten, and a living testament to the power of faith, love, and perseverance.

"Twice I faced the storm, and twice I emerged stronger. My story isn't just about surviving—it's about thriving, loving fiercely, and using every ounce of my journey to uplift others. Together, we are unstoppable."

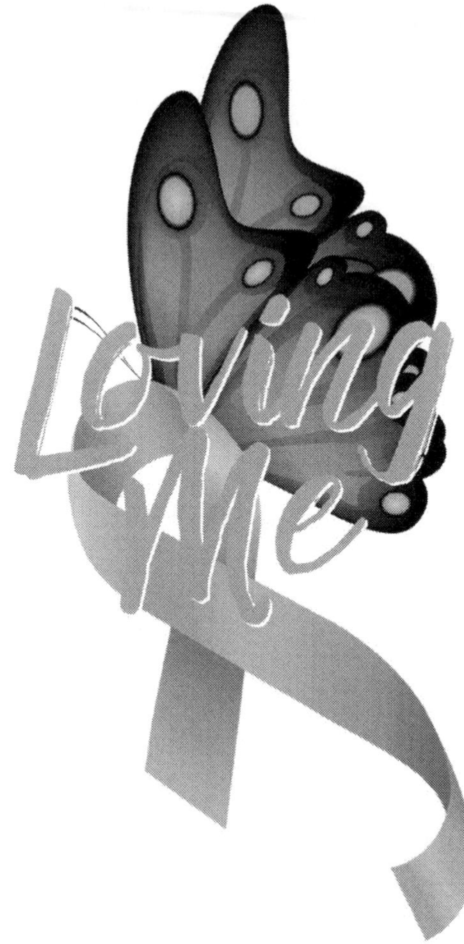
Loving Me

shero.
Publishing
SHEROPUBLISHING.COM

Made in the USA
Columbia, SC
20 June 2025